Insurance Billing 101

for Massage Therapists

Julie Onofrio, LMP

Insurance Billing 101 for Massage Therapists

Copyright © 2012 by Julie Onofrio, LMP
Pine Woods Publishing LLC.

All rights reserved. No part of this book may be reproduced or transmitted in any form or by any means without written permission of the author.

This book/ebook is designed to provide accurate information on insurance billing for massage therapists. It is sold with the understanding that the Publisher/Author is not engaged in rendering legal, accounting or other professional services and if you need legal or accounting assistance, you will need to contact a professional.

Insurance Billing 101 for Massage Therapists, Pine Woods Publishing LLC/ Julie Onofrio, LMP, is not responsible for your direct or indirect results that may come from the use of this information.

ISBN-10: 0983977615
ISBN-13: 978-0-9839776-1-2

Table of Contents

Introduction..2

Chapter One. Bill Insurance for Massage- Yes or NO?...............................12

Chapter Two. HIPAA. Health Insurance Portability and Accountability Act.........20

Chapter Three. What to Charge for Your Massage Services......................25

Chapter Four. Types of Insurance (Overview) 31

Chapter Five. Personal Injury : Motor Vehicle Collisions and Other Accidents.......35

Chapter Six. Private Health Insurance : HMO's, PPO's, Affinity Plans..................40

Chapter Seven. Worker's Compensation or Labor and Industries.............................44

Chapter Eight. CMS – 1500. The Billing Form Explained.........................46

Chapter Nine. CPT Codes and ICD-9 Codes..52

Chapter Ten. Documentation. SOAP Notes, Progress Reports, Narrative Reports. 56

Chapter Eleven. Getting Paid and What to do if You Don't Get Paid.......................63

Chapter Twelve. Networking to Build Your Practice..................................67

Chapter Thirteen. Putting It All Together..72

Chapter Fourteen. The Challenges of Billing. 79

Chapter Fifteen. Getting More Health Insurance to Pay............................84

Chapter Sixteen. Hiring a Billing Person..90

Chapter Seventeen. Glossary. 91

Resources:...107

Index..124

To all those who choose to
accept the challenge of billing insurance: You are stepping up for the profession and making a difference for all.

Billing Insurance is different in each state and within each plan. It is up to you to take this information and apply it to whatever insurance company you are working with. You will need to ask the insurance company, the client/patient, the doctors and attorneys questions in order to bill and get paid. I also suggest that you find a mentor to help you through the process and then help others and pass the information on.

Introduction

This Insurance Billing Manual was first released in 2005 as an ebook online on my website – www.thebodyworker.com . Since then it has gone through many changes and I offered the information for free on my website but I decided to republish it to share what I have learned about insurance billing because it has been a mainstay in my massage business and has helped me make a good living for 23 years. I have been a Massage Therapist in Washington State since 1989 and billed my massage services to insurance companies right from the very start. My initial training of 250 hours in basic massage allowed me to bill for car accidents and for job related injuries. (At the time, 250 hours was all that Washington State was required to become a licensed massage practitioner.) I have been lucky to live in a progressive state where massage has been widely accepted. In about 1996 a law was created in WA State called the "Every Category Law" (http://apps.leg.wa.gov/wac/default.aspx?cite=284-43-205) that allowed WA State Massage Therapists to become contracted providers with the major medical insurance companies such as Regence Blue Shield and Aetna. The law was created because we were fortunate to have a very savvy insurance commissioner named Debra Senn who believed in massage. Her massage therapist, Lori Belinski was very active for the massage profession at the time (and is now the Executive Director Washington State Chiropractic Association). It was the right combination to make things happen. The insurance companies protested the law by holding it up in court until January 1999, when the US Supreme Court put an end to the dispute. The law is still challenged every year in some way but continues to survive.

I immediately applied and was accepted, as a contracted provider, into many of the major medical insurance companies. Contracts with the insurance companies dictate what you can and cannot bill for, what CPT (Current Procedural Terminology) codes you can use, and how much they will pay for each code. In the beginning most companies paid the amount that I billed bringing constant revenue to my massage business. Each year they pay less and less, but you will still get clients just by being on the list of providers so it makes the process of getting clients much easier.

Back in 1989, there were not any classes on massage insurance billing, so I had to learn to interact with insurance companies, doctors and clients through networking with other massage therapists and constantly figuring out how to bill insurance for massage. There was one simple manual on Massage Insurance Billing created by Chris Roche that helped me get started. We learned mainly through trial and error and sharing what worked and what didn't work.

Through the years, there have been many changes in the world of massage insurance billing. Plans are constantly changing and more insurance companies are paying for massage services. Finally it has become easier to get paid with the creation of free electronic billing services like www.officeally.com .

Washington is still the only state, to my knowledge, that allows and even mandates that Massage Therapists become contracted providers with insurance companies. A contracted provider is one who applies to the insurance company to be under contract with them and they must pass a credentialing process that mainly is about your work history and does not require any additional training or technique classes. There are many companies in each state who allow providers to pay for massage services without having to be contracted providers. Florida has a law that says insurance companies must pay for massage but, in that state, massage therapists are not under contract with insurance companies. Being able to bill insurance companies for massage helps make massage more available for injuries and various health conditions. It helps make it more affordable for people who do need it for their health.

Unfortunately, as massage therapists under contract, we are not able to negotiate with insurance companies or try to ask for better reimbursement. We also cannot boycott or protest current contracts as doing so would violate contract laws and anti-trust laws, according to the AMTA - WA attorneys. So basically we have to just abide by the rules and fees that the insurance companies set.

Massage Therapists in other states wish they could be contracted providers or at least be able to bill health insurance companies. Billing auto insurance and workers compensation plans can also supplement a massage therapist's income and help keep clients coming so that they can stay in business. There is also talk of the new Affordable Healthcare Act that was created by the Obama administration may help massage therapists in every state be able to bill insurance. This is the reason for my creating this manual for massage therapists: to help you decide if you want to learn how to bill or get involved with billing; to start exposing you to insurance companies vocabulary and how billing works; to suggest how to interact with insurance companies and the health care profession; to gain insight into becoming more recognized by insurance companies, doctors, health care professionals and the general public. The more we can learn about the insurance process as a profession, the more we will be able to learn what is needed to help our profession be more recognized as a health care provider and help people support their health. The best way to change the system is to be a part of it and to participate by speaking up and working toward change. Therefore, we need more massage therapists who know how to bill and understand the issues of billing so we can do just that.

The information provided here is as accurate as I can make it from my experience with billing in WA State. While I can not really tell you everything you specifically need to know in your area, I hope that this will get you thinking about billing insurance and start taking small steps in learning more. Each state and each company will have their own unique plans and rules and regulations for billing. You will have to discover what works best for you and what is taking place in your state. You will be responsible for working with each insurance company and finding the right answers to be able to work with clients and bill their insurance for massage and get paid. Since each policy, plan and insurance company and each state have different licensing laws, scope of practice laws and billing procedures, there is no way that I can really tell you how to bill insurance for your individual situation. What I can do is give you information that will at help you learn to ask the right questions and give you the tools and knowledge to help solve the issues that you will face when you bill insurance for massage services. I have also created a insurance billing forum (http://massagepracticebuilder.com/massage-insurance-billing/forum) on my website **www.massagepracticebuilder.com** where I highly recommend that you find a mentor or be a mentor to others in your area. The forum shares information about what is going on in your area, how to get massage to be more accepted by insurance, and how to bill for massage in your area.

Billing insurance is still a mixed blessing for me. Yes, we can bill insurance. Insurance work can bring in more clients, help stabilize a massage business, and help it grow. Insurance has supported me for 23 years. I have been able to help people who are in pain and under stress dealing with injuries and conditions that massage can help. On the other hand, billing insurance is a big challenge in many ways – both financially and mentally/emotionally. It has been the biggest ethical challenge of my career as you will learn later in this book. Again, all issues can be managed with the help and support of others in the profession.

The process of billing insurance companies for your massage therapy services will be time consuming and often challenging. Each state and each insurance company in each state will require different paperwork and will use different codes and will reimburse different amounts for the same CPT code. Within each company, you will often find that procedures vary greatly from policy to policy. I can guarantee that no matter how many manuals you read or classes you take on billing that you will still have problems collecting the money that is owed to you. Just expect it and you won't be bothered by it. In order to reduce the headaches that you will get, you need to know the right questions to ask the insurance company, the client, the attorney and anyone else involved so that you can get paid. In order to know what questions you need to ask, you need to learn everything you can about the insurance industry and how to communicate effectively about what it is you are doing with each client. Working with insurance companies will be a constant learning experience. It will be a process that will challenge you to learn more and ask more for yourself. You will find yourself needing patience, strong boundaries and the willingness to take a stand for yourself.

With this in mind, I write this guide with the intention of providing you with the basic information that you will need to know to start working with insurance companies, physicians and attorneys. After you decide whether to accept the challenge of insurance billing you will need to know what codes you can bill for, how to fill out a CMS 1500 billing form and have a good idea about what you can do if you are not getting paid. The key to working with insurance companies is to learn what questions to ask.

Some of the challenges you will be faced with include:

- Being asked to reduce your fees for your services
- Waiting 1 month to 3 years for payment
- Having to call each month to see where the check is
- Having to call to see why the payment has been denied
- Resubmitting bills because they were lost or incorrect and waiting another month or so for payment
- Waiting on hold to talk to a customer service representative
- Being told the check is in the mail – again
- Learning what you need to do with each company in order to get paid
- Having to deal with clients/patients who think massage is for maintenance of their health when it generally is not. There are very few plans that have wellness massage benefits.
- Being asked to take a lower fee even after you have done everything and they are owning you a substantial amount of money.

Chapter One asks the question – Do you want to bill for insurance? Billing isn't for everyone and it is really more of a math question. Will billing help your business be profitable?

Chapters 2-7 will teach you the basics about the different types of insurance coverage. Motor vehicle accidents, Provider Networks and worker's compensation.

Chapter 8 deals with the billing form that is used by most carriers the CMS 1500 and how to fill it out correctly to get paid faster.

Chapter 9 covers the codes that you will need to know to be able to fill out the form correctly.

Chapter 10 teaches how to chart a client's progress and show improvement.

Chapter 11 is some of the tricks you need to be aware of to get paid.

Chapter 12 teaches you how to build a network of referrals.

Chapter 13 is a list of the questions you will need to ask the insurance company, the client and the attorney to help eliminate problems in getting paid.

Chapter 14 is about the many challenges you will be faced with.

Chapter 15 is some ideas for becoming a contracted provider or get health insurance companies to pay for massage.

At the end is a complete glossary of terms to help you learn what the insurance companies are talking about.

The appendix has a chart for figuring out your cost per client, intake forms, insurance verification forms, progress reports, billing tracking form, a link ICD-9 codes commonly used and a list of resources for more information on billing insurance companies.

While I have tried to provide the most accurate information that I have, insurance billing is complicated and challenging. You will have to keep up to date with the changes yourself and know the laws and rules for billing in your state. I hope that this guide will help you to start the billing process and start learning what questions to ask the insurance companies, clients/patients, doctors, lawyers, insurance adjusters and representatives. I also feel that the more people that learn how to bill and understand what is going on in the world of billing insurance, that when the profession is faced with new laws and political battles for the right to bill that more people will get involved to protect and preserve our right to bill insurance.

Please join me on this journey into the world of massage insurance billing.

Julie Onofrio, LMP

Seattle, WA

Chapter One. Bill Insurance for Massage- Yes or NO?

At some time in your career in massage, you will be asked to bill insurance for a long time client or friend. You might also think about taking insurance if you need more clients or are looking for ways to supplement your income and also sustain you through a changing economy. Billing Insurance for massage therapy services can help supplement your income and give you a steady flow of clients. You can also choose to have a business that does only insurance cases. It requires more time and energy to bill an insurance company and get paid. Some insurance companies will pay what you bill and others will pay less than you bill. You will have to decide for yourself if billing insurance will help make your massage business more profitable. It is part just doing the math and part ethics – will billing insurance fit into you vision for your massage business and the type of massage you do.

You will need to ask yourself some questions that may help you decide:

- Will it help your massage business be more profitable?
- Is the best use of your time? You will to be spending more time doing paperwork, networking with doctors

and dealing with insurance companies. Will you be making enough money to cover that extra time?
- Do you need more clients in general? Is your business slow and do you need clients? Are you looking to grow and hire massage therapists as employees or independent contractors?
- Are others in your area billing insurance successfully?
- Do you want to be involved in having massage be more accepted by the medical community which may mean becoming politically active in your community?
- Do you know how to do clinical (medical) massage or are willing to learn?
- Are you interested in research and learning to use it to promote your massage business and the massage profession?

The first thing to decide is what the potential profits will be from taking insurance clients. You can calculate that by looking at your cost per client using the following formula:

1. Compute your office overhead for a month:
   Take the last 12 months and divide by 12 or if you are just starting out, use what statistics you have.

Salary	
Rent	
Other Salaries	
Equipment Leases	

Tables	
Malpractice Insurance	
Licensing Fees	
Lotions/Oils	
Sheets	
Laundry	
Music	
Utilities	
Office Supplies	
Water	
Magazines	
Books	
Copies	
Billing Services	
Association Fees	
Marketing	
Advertising	
Totals:	

2. Compute the number of patients for the month. You can use a number from last year's patients divided by 12 or estimate the number for this year.

3. Cost per patient = Total monthly expenses____ divided by Total monthly patient visits _____

4. Evaluate:

- If you are planning on joining a HMO or PPO, what is the expected income per treatment? Is it higher than the cost per patient or less than the cost per patient/client?

- How much will your cost per patient vary when the number of clients increases due to becoming a member?
- Will you have an increased volume of clients that will make the cost per client less?
- Will you get too many clients and therefore have to hire office support to do the extra paper and telephone work?
- Will accepting insurance clients be in tune with your personal and business mission statement? (Do you have a mission statement?)
- Do you need clients to fill your schedule?
- Are you willing to learn about how to bill, take chart notes, work with doctors and with clients in their treatments and in getting paid?
- Are you willing to stand up in court or legal proceedings and testify or give a deposition for your clients? (You usually get paid to do so but it is time consuming.)

In some states, you will need to find out if other massage therapists are billing insurance companies and which companies they are billing. I have created an online forum (http://massagepracticebuilder.com/forum/) to help you do that or you can start looking for other massage therapists in your area to ask if they are billing insurance successfully. It still will be a learning process, but you can do it together and make it less painful!

You may also have to see if the insurance company has any specific rules for being able to bill insurance companies. One common problem is that some insurance com- panies will only pay for massage when it is done by a chiropractor or physical therapist or under the care of one of those providers. You will need to check to see what is needed for each plan and each client/patient.

Some of the other challenges with billing insurance such as the extra time it takes to do all of the paperwork needs to be considered also. You will spend time marketing to doctors and talking with lawyers. In working with insurance, you will also be limited to working on specific injury areas and will have to learn how to write effective chart notes so that you will get paid and show that your sessions are showing improvement. You will spend time writing progress reports and may even be called to testify at a mediation, arbitration or in court.

Working with insurance companies will also challenge your integrity and boundaries at times. I have been told by insurance companies to do things like "Just make up an ICD-9 (diagnosis code)" which it is illegal since massage therapists are not allowed to make a diagnosis. Clients will often try to get more massage than is actually needed and they sometimes will embellish their symptoms to get more treatments. They also will try to come for maintenance massage which is usually not covered by most plans or in most situations. (I have only seen a few preventative plans that allow this.) Having an accurate pain and movement tracking system can help you show improvement and avoid doing maintenance massage which is generally not allowed when billing insurances. Insurance will often not cover a full recovery from an accident or injury, but will only cover people until they return to work and are fully functional – there is a difference. Some people can be functional but will still be in quite a bit of pain. You may also be asked to reduce your rates when it comes time to settle the claim if the money has been used up in other areas by first paying doctors and surgeons.

If you decide that you do want to continue, you must learn everything you can about insurance and billing. It will help you set boundaries and choose what clients you want to work with. As you learn more and work with more cases, you will be able to tell which cases will be most difficult to settle or prove medical necessity. You can choose not to work with any that you find are questionable or will take up too much time and not be worth the extra time. This is one of the most overlooked keys to building a successful practice. Sacrificing your values and accepting money just to make money when it goes against your values will create stress and increase your risk of burnout. You don't have to accept every client who calls. You can focus on working on clients who value your work and are compatible with your beliefs.

While you can have a successful massage business without billing insurance companies, knowing how to bill will come in handy when your favorite client gets in a motor vehicle accident (MVA) and wants you to bill the insurance company for him/her. You can also build a practice totally dependent on insurance cases and work with integrity when you know all the rules, regulations and issues. Just be sure you have a backup plan in case one of the income from billing ends unexpectedly. Will you be able to stay in business if the laws change or you are suddenly unable to bill a certain area of insurance like Personal Injury or Worker's Compensation?

Here in WA when we are contracted providers with insurance companies, we are placed on a list of providers. This can be an easy way to get clients. People will just look for a provider in their area and then may just look for you online to see if you are a good match for their needs. They may also just call you right away. Insurance clients may come to you once a week or even twice a week, depending on the injury and the prescription from the doctor. Having regular clients means having regular income, which is one of the top reasons for taking insurance. People may also visit you more frequently when covered by insurance. Taking insurance can help fill your schedule with clients. Keeping insurance cases balanced out with your regular work can be a great way to create a sustainable practice. Taking cases where you have to wait to be paid can be like putting money in the bank if you are able to manage your budget while you wait.

And Remember… You can also opt not to take insurance even though you may feel the pressure from clients and the profession to jump on the bandwagon. You can successfully create a totally cash based massage business. But that will take probably the same amount of energy to market and promote yourself as it does to deal with the insurance companies. It also does not have to be an either or thing. You can bill for some clients and have an even mixture of cash and insurance billing. Actually, that is what I would recommend that you do so as to not put all of your eggs in one basket!

Chapter Two. HIPAA. Health Insurance Portability and Accountability Act.

The Health Insurance Portability and Accountability Act or HIPAA, was implemented in April 2003. It was created as a result of the internet and electronic billing and communications in an effort to protect people's privacy. HIPAA protects and enhances the rights of consumers by providing them with access to their health information and controlling inappropriate use of their information. It is an effort to improve consumers trust in the health care system and improve the efficiency and effectiveness of health care delivery. HIPAA is what requires you to sign a form saying you read and signed a form about your rights to privacy!

The general rule is that you only have to be HIPAA Compliant if you exchanged information electronically or in other words billed insurances electronically. Even if you are not using electronic systems to communicate with insurance companies and clients, it is still a good idea to be aware of your client's rights to privacy. If you work with doctors who are required to be HIPAA Compliant, you also are required to be HIPAA Compliant because of what is called "the chain of trust" in the insurance world.

Figuring out what needs to be done to be HIPAA Compliant for a massage therapist requires that you take some time to read the information on the US Department of Health and Human Services Website on Health Information Privacy (http://www.hhs.gov/ocr/privacy/). Someone in your office will need to be made in charge of figuring it all out and becoming HIPAA compliant meaning you, if you are self employed and are the only one!

You can also just really use some common sense and think about the client and what information they are giving you and what it all really means. *Everything* that a client tells you should be confidential even without HIPAA.

Here are some things that you will need to know about and complete.

- Create a manual for your office outlining all of your policies regarding client care and privacy issues.
- Create a document that will inform clients of your policies that they will sign. (*Notification of Privacy Policies – NOPP*). Have them initial another form saying that they have received their NOPP. (see https://sohnen-moe.com/forms.php)
- Clients are entitled to see a copy of their records.
- Create a *statement of privacy* and how you will use client information or potential client information on your website. (see https://sohnen-moe.com/forms.php)

- Have clients fill out an *informed consent form* telling them what will happen in the massage session. (see https://sohnen-moe.com/forms.php)
- Have a separate locked, fireproof file cabinet for storage of files and/or a secure computer access.
- If you collect clients email addresses and other personal contact information for marketing purposes, you will need to inform them that is why you are collecting the info.
- Don't let clients look at your appointment books or other client files or data. If your appointment book is sitting on the counter while booking a client, keep the book out of their sight.
- If you are calling a client, make sure that no one else hears the name of the person that you are calling.
- Put notices of confidentiality on emails and faxes.
- Clients have the right to object to the massage therapist's privacy policy and in turn the Massage therapist has the right to deny treatment.

While this list is not complete, it will help you get started in becoming HIPAA compliant.

You can find the forms that you will need on www.sohnen-moe.com -the website of Cherie Sohnen-Moe, author of *Business Mastery* and the *Ethics of Touch*.

If you are billing insurance companies electronically you will need what is called a National Provider Identification Number. It is free through the National Plan and Provider Enumeration System (NPPES) https://nppes.cms.hhs.gov/NPPES/Welcome.do

To obtain the number – fill out the form at the address above. You will use taxonomy number category 22 – restorative therapy/massage therapy. Massage Therapist **225700000X**

You will need to have the following information to fill out the form.

Information Required for Individual Providers (From their website)
Provider Name
SSN (or ITIN if not eligible for SSN)
Provider Date of Birth
Country of Birth
State of Birth(if Country of Birth is U.S.)
Provider Gender
Mailing Address
Practice Location Address and Phone Number
Taxonomy (Provider Type)
State License Information
Contact Person Name
Contact Person Phone Number and E-mail

See also:

US Dept. of Health and Human Services (http://www.hhs.gov/ocr/privacy/index.html) – Health Information Privacy

Everything You Ever Wanted to Know About HIPAA (http://www.massagetoday.com/archives/2003/01/05.html) An Interview With HIPAA Authority Howard Ross Massage Today January, 2003, Vol. 03, Issue 01

Living the Law An Update on HIPAA (http://www.massageandbodywork.com/Articles/DecJan2004/HIPAA.html) By Cherie Sohnen-Moe. Massage and Bodywork Magazine

Susan Salvo's reply to a question on HIPAA on www.massageprofessionals.com (http://www.massageprofessionals.com/forum/topics/hippa-forms-and-other-forms?commentId=2887274:Comment:92010)

HIPAA Plain & Simple: (book on amazon.com) A Healthcare Professionals Guide to Achieve HIPAA and HITECH Compliance (http://www.amazon.com/gp/product/1603592059/ref=as_li_ss_tl?ie=UTF8&tag=thebodyworkercom&linkCode=as2&camp=1789&creative=390957&creativeASIN=1603592059

Chapter Three. What to Charge for Your Massage Services.

Knowing what you can charge an insurance company is a legal matter and an ethical issue. Many massage therapists think that when they bill insurance companies they will be able to charge more for their services to the insurance companies. In general, insurance companies will pay more than a cash client. Figuring out what to charge insurance companies for your services is a challenge because there are many differing opinions. I can't tell you what you should charge. Most massage therapists think that you will be able to charge more than your usual fee –your usual cash rate - because it takes more time to process the bills, do the chart notes, talk to the insurance companies and everything else that goes along with working with injured clients and their insurance companies. Most automobile insurance companies will pay more for each session, but that does not mean that you can charge more. The issue lies with setting your fees to begin with. Charge what you need to make for each session. When you bill an insurance company, you use a code that designates the type of massage you are doing. The insurance company will pay you per unit of massage, which is a 15-minute increment. So if you charge $60 per hour, your fees would be $15 per unit (4x15=60). Insurance companies may also limit the number of units you can bill in one day. Some will pay for hour sessions and some for an hour and a half session and some that don't pay for the full hour.

The insurance industry has created called the Usual, Customary and Reasonable (UCR) fee created by the National Fee Analyzer. (http://www.shopingenix.com/Product/37403/) Surveys of what massage therapists are being paid by different companies are averaged out per area and are called the UCR. Some massage therapists think that they can just charge the UCR rate. The problem is that it is illegal to charge an insurance company more for your services than a cash client, when you are doing the same type of massage. Managed care plans (such as a PPO or HMO) are not subject to reasonable and customary fees, meaning they don't have to pay the UCR. (You can find out what the UCR is in your area by searching on the American Medical Association Website at https://commerce.ama-assn.org/store/index.jsp)

The AMTA-WA attorneys, Pieck and Conniff, had a class on this a few years ago and stressed that if you charge more to insurance companies than you do to your regular cash clients – it is considered insurance fraud - which is punishable by jail time and a hefty fine. There are many reasons used to justify charging more to the insurance company. They explain it more in their article on their website "The Business Side of Caring" (PDF) (http://www.peicklaw.com/PDF/The%20Business%20of%20Caring.pdf

Massage therapists in the class explained:

"We have so much paperwork to do that takes time".

"We do different massage techniques when we are working on insurance clients".

"It takes so long to get paid."

Whatever your reason, should you decide to charge more, be prepared to prove it in court. Courts do not really care if there is paperwork or it takes more time to get paid. It is just part of doing business. If you are doing a different technique, you will have to be able to show that you do something different on an insurance client than you do on a cash client. If a client came in with an injury and paid cash would you be doing something different to treat this person and would you be charging a different rate?

Diana Thompson author of *"Hands Heal"* (a book on how to write chart notes) has said that you may be able to charge the extra fee that you pay a person to do your billing. Thompson also says:

> "It is illegal to charge different rates for the same service to different people or organizations. It is appropriate however, to charge different fees for different services or to offer reasonable discounts for payment on the day of service as long as the discount is offered to all patients equally."

So if you pay a billing person $15 for each bill they submit for you, you can add that into the fee. If your cash rate is $65 an hour, you can then charge $80. (This is just an example.)

Another way people justify a difference in charge is by saying that they offer cash clients a discount because they pay cash. You may be able to call it a payment at the time of service discount. You will need to check with your attorney if this is allowed in your area.

According to this information, if you are working on a cash client and using a technique that would be billed as code 97124 – you must charge your insurance rate to your cash client. You have to charge the same amount for the same service regardless of who is paying.

To further confuse the issue, David Luther who wrote a book on insurance billing in 2001 and found that you can indeed charge more for your sessions because of all the paperwork involved. He says:

> "A medical equipment retailer wanted to "charge Medicare prices which are higher than it charges retail customers for the same products." The OIG's Advisory Opinion 98-8 re: Discounts states:
>
> "if the higher costs are 'due to unusual circumstances or medical complications requiring additional time, effort, expense or other good cause,' due to claims processing, documentation… and delays/denials in Medicare payment, then suppliers are allowed to charge Medicare more than their 'usual charge'."
>
> Because insurance industry standards very often comply with Medicare standards, the OIG's opinion may be applicable to

all medical massage in- surance claims. Whether patients pay you directly or insurance pays you, prescribed medical massage still requires considerably more time, effort and expense than non-medical massage." (See except at http://www.handsontrade.com/Articles/MedMsgArticle/MedMsgArtforInsWebsite.htm and the http://oig.hhs.gov/fraud/docs/advisoryopinions/1998/ao98_8.pdf)

So how do you set your fees for sessions that you bill to insurance? Who really knows what is legal? Ethical is a whole other story. Some massage therapists charge insurance companies in excess of $200 for an hour session. I have even heard as high as $400. When massage therapists charge that much for a session it confuses the clients as well as hurts the massage profession. Insurance companies who see those rates will eventually get wise and reduce rates for everyone. That is happening right now in FL with a law being passed that will take away the ability to bill for car accident (PIP) insurance due to over-billing and fraud in the insurance world and possibly some interesting politics.

You need to set your fees in order to make a living, pay the bills, save for retirement and grow your massage business. I was once told to set my fees so that I don't feel resentful when I work with a client and that has seemed to hold up no matter what the situation. A big problem is that many massage therapists struggle financially so when they see an opportunity to charge more, they will find reasons to make the extra charge work.

So part of the problem I see, is that we are hesitant to charge what we need to make to be successful and make a great living in the first place. If you think an insurance company should be paying you $150 an hour, then why don't you think that a cash client should be paying you the same? Just because it is an insurance company and that they are large enough to absorb the fees or that they won't care? This may be an indication of the inherent problems in the massage profession more than the issue of insurance billing.

The way to set your fees is to determine what you need to make each month and then looking at how many massages you want to do each month and divide. If you need to make $5,000 a month and the average number of clients you want to see in a month is 75 (that is about 18 a week) then your hourly fee should be around $65 per hour. If you need to see X amount of clients each month, then you can set your marketing goals accordingly and work to make that happen. If you can't get enough clients at that rate, then you might have to adjust your fees and lower your rates to get new clients. There are also adverse affects to that. If others in your area are charging more than you and you are undercutting everyone else with the intent to take clients away from others, you might want to look at your business ethics. You are a valuable asset to the profession and worth the rate that you need to charge. Working with a supervisor or mentor can help you take the steps to raise your self confidence and your rates!

Chapter Four. Types of Insurance (Overview)

In general, there are three instances where insurance companies can be billed for your services:

- Motor Vehicle accidents (MVA), also known as motor vehicle collisions (MVC) or other accidents such as slipping and falling. Accidents are also now being called incidents or being referred to as a motor vehicle collision so that fault is not implied.
- Worker's compensation (WC) (sometimes known as Labor & Industries or L&I) which involves injuries that happen while a person is at work.
- Private health insurance companies such as a Health Maintenance Organization (HMO) or Preferred Provider Organization (PPO).

Motor vehicle accidents (collisions) and Personal Injury allow payments for services that are medically necessary. Massage Therapy in most states is recognized as being medically necessary by the auto insurance industry as long as you can verify treatment and show improvement. Auto insurance policies, for the most part, will pay the fees that you charge, if all paperwork is in order. FL massage therapist will not be able to bill PIP after Dec 2012 (or it could be in July 2012. There is some confusion over the date as I write this.)

Personal Injury Insurance. Part of an insurance policy that covers bodily and property damage. Can be a car insurance policy, a homeowners policy or commercial building insurance policy. The most common is a Motor Vehicle Accident (MVA) or more currently being referred to as a motor vehicle collision (MVC).

Personal injury protection (PIP) or **Med-Pay (MP) PIP** is part of an automobile insurance policy that is purchased separately with varied limits and coverage. Each state is different but here in Washington State, it is a required part of the policy. Also in WA, a person can elect not to purchase PIP coverage, if they can prove they have other health insurance coverage and if they sign a waiver rejecting the PIP. PIP policies usually have a time limit for which services can be billed. Each state varies. When it comes time to settle the case, your services will come under scrutiny by lawyers and the insurance companies involved. Med-Pay is the no fault insurance version of PIP. The benefits will pay for all medical needs no matter who is at fault for the accident. PIP will pay for your clients' medical treatment until it is time to settle the case or the benefits run out.

- **Third party coverage/liability**. This refers to the liability coverage of the party who is at fault. Some companies will pay directly when it is clear who is at fault. Other times you may have to wait until the liability is determined and the case is settled, which may be up to the time limit which varies state to state (i.e.- 1-3 years). You are usually paid when the case is settled. Cases can be settled with or without a lawyer. Lawyers are usually involved when there are complicated injuries and property damage. Cases may be settled using arbitration, mediation, or jury trials. Developing a good working relationship with a law firm will increase your chances of getting paid. It is advisable to file a health care lien (more about liens later) to increase your chances of getting paid. Often you can charge interest while you are waiting to be paid. You can also charge for making copies of chart notes and other things in the client's file when they are requested by the third party or lawyer. There may be legal limits as to what you can charge for copies.

- **Uninsured motorists.** When the party who caused the accident is at fault and they don't have any car insurance, the accident is covered by the injured parties uninsured motorist protection. They usually pay for damages and injuries up front and get the money later from the party at fault.

Private health insurance – includes managed care plans (PPO-Preferred Provider Organizations, HMO-Health Maintenance Organizations) major medical, Medicare and Medicaid.

- Indemnity plans or fee-for service – type of plan where the insurance companies pay fees for the services provided to the insured people covered by the policy. You go to the doctor and do whatever is necessary and the bill is sent to the insurance company.

- Managed Care Plans: include Preferred Provider Organizations (PPO), Health Maintenance Organizations (HMO). Washington is the only state that officially allows massage therapists to become a contracted provider. In FL, massage therapists are also able to bill health insurance but they are not contracted providers. This does not mean that you won't be able to get paid by such organizations in your area. It will require extra efforts to prove that you work can save the company money in the long run. Many insurers will 'willingly pay' meaning that they will pay even though they don't have to.

- Private Health Insurance: includes Major medical, Medicare and Medicaid plans. **Medicare and Medicaid *do not*** pay for massage therapy services at this time.

Worker's compensation or Labor and Industries- ALL Injuries that happen at work must be sent through the worker's compensation plan or Labor and Industries whichever it is in your state. This will include a motor vehicle accident that occurs while working. Often other insurance coverage such as a PPO will deny payment when an injury is due to a work situation. There are usually limits to treatments times, number of sessions and who can provide the treatments. You may have to apply to become a provider in each state and abide by the provider contracts. The goal is usually to get the worker back to work as soon as possible. There are limits to the policies. Each of these types of insurance is explained further in their own chapter.

Chapter Five. Personal Injury : Motor Vehicle Collisions and Other Accidents

Massage Therapy has been shown to markedly affect the healing time of injuries due to motor vehicle collisions. Since massage therapists are not qualified to make a diagnosis, it is necessary to have a referral/prescription from the treating physician. Some insurance companies will tell you it is not needed. I would advise getting one in **any** situation. This protects you if the case ever goes to court, arbitration or mediation.

The first thing you need to determine is which insurance company is paying. Often the client's Personal Injury Protection (PIP) or Medpay (MP) will pay for your services within 30-90 days. This is one of the most common and profitable for massage therapists as payment is usually made without delays or questions about things such as fees. These policies usually have dollar limits and time limits for treatments. You will also have to bill within a certain time frame and each insurance company is different so you must ask when you start to bill. If you delay sending bills past the time limit, you may be out of money without any recourse. If treatments extend beyond the policy's limit, the patient must start a claim with their insurance company. When those benefits are exhausted, the claim is usually resolved in a settlement from the insurance company of the party at fault. You can still treat the client but you won't get paid until the case settles. Such cases can prove to be risky to take on. This often involves lawyers, for each party negotiating the settlement. Laws vary from state to state regarding statue of limitations, settlements etc.

If there isn't any PIP or Medpay, you may have to wait to be paid until the case settles. It may take as long as three years depending on what regulations your state has for such cases. This means you will need to be able to wait for payment. You may be able to apply simple interest as set by your state for health care providers. You will have to find out the information yourself by searching the health care providers laws in your state.

Liens. A lien is a written agreement between the involved parties (lawyers, the massage therapist and the client) to ensure that payments will be made when the case is settled. Each state has specific rules about where to file the lien. You may only need to file a lien if you take a third party claim or if PIP benefits or Med-Pay benefits run out and you have to wait to be paid until the case settles. Check with your attorney or your county clerk's office to determine what needs to be done to file a lien in your state. It could be with the county auditor, the lawyers' office and/or the patient depending on what is required. Send a copy of the lien to the client, both insurance companies and any attorneys that are involved. After the case is settled, you have to remove the lien or the client will have credit problems. Settlement could take 1-3 years or more depending on the statue of limitations in your state. You will not get paid until the case settles. You can choose not to accept cases that will delay payment for such a long time or ask that the client pay as they go. Liens may have expiration dates that also need to be monitored and renewed if necessary. They also may need to be filed within a certain time frame from when the collision occurred. Check with your state laws.

Working with lawyers. Building a professional relationship with a few personal injury lawyers in your area may be beneficial while building your practice. Lawyers can help clients find the right health care practitioners. I had a client who was such a lawyer when I first started out in business. He connected me with a chiropractor who then often referred clients to me for treatment. You might want to invite attorneys and chiropractors in so that you can work on them or directly market your massage business to them so they will become clients. You can also contact local law firms with a letter of introduction and some business cards or fliers. They are usually looking for contacts to build their business.

Call the attorney when you begin working with a client to find out what they will require of you as far as paperwork, insurance benefits and settlements. Most attorneys have legal assistants that can be of great help to you when it comes to getting paid. You can write a letter to each attorney and introduce yourself and ask them what they will need from you. You may be required to send copies of the bills, copies of chart notes and copies of the prescriptions for massage therapy. You will need to have the client sign a release of records form to allow you to send medical records to each party involved.

It is not necessary for all clients that have been in a MVA to retain a lawyer. A client may wish to hire a lawyer if the injuries are severe, if the client can't work due to the injuries or if there are difficulties getting the providers paid or settling the case. Cases can be settled without attorneys. It is up to the individual.

Attorneys can also be influential in getting the doctor to refer the injured party to massage therapists. Most attorneys get paid based on a percentage of the settlement. While they often may have the clients' health in mind, they may also want to increase the amount of the bills to increase their income from the settlement. I recommend working with physicians and attorneys who have the same values as you do when it comes to this issue.

There may be some time in your career that you will have to appear in court or in an arbitration or mediation to determine the settlement. You will be able to charge for your appearance. You will also have to be prepared and have detailed progress notes to help prove medical necessity and how the injuries have impacted the clients' life and health. You will need to keep your files up to date and in order.

IME'S- Clients in a MVA or other accident may be asked by their insurance companies to go to an Independent Medical exam (IME) to confirm their injuries and healing progress. The insurance company often makes this request when they think that the case is becoming too expensive. They will then place limits on treatments and will need stringent verification of activities. From what I have seen, this usually means they are trying to settle the case. The client is sent to a doctor that usually works for the insurance company. They have the right to be examined by a physician that has the same credentials as the referring physician. (If the referring physician is a chiropractor, the IME doctor should be a chiropractor.) Treatment is most often terminated, but occasionally more tests are requested and sessions can be extended.

I highly recommend that the client retain an attorney if an IME is called for to protect the clients' rights. Often someone from the attorney's office may accompany the client to the IME. If a person refuses to go to an IME, benefits are usually automatically terminated.

Uninsured Motorists Protection is the insurance coverage that protects the policy holder when they have been involved in an accident and the other party does not have insurance or covers you when the person leaves the scene of the accident. It can pay you up front or may not pay until the claim is settled. Be sure to ask the insurance company when it is that you will be getting paid.

Slip and Fall accidents, pedestrian/vehicle accidents may also be covered by insurance. Home owners insurance may pay for an injured party's treatment as in cases where someone may slip and fall or have some other kind of accident on another person's property. Car insurance will also pay in situations that involve a motorist/pedestrian (walking/biking) on the street.

Chapter Six. Private Health Insurance : HMO's, PPO's, Affinity Plans

Private health insurance includes a variety of companies and plans, such as managed care plans (HMO's, PPO's). These organizations contract with providers who agree to work with their members at a specific contracted rate and under their strict regulations. Washington is the only state that mandates that massage therapists to be contracted providers through the "Every Category Law". A contracted provider goes through a credentialing process with the insurance company and signs a contract that stipulates what they must do to get paid and they must accept the 'allowable fee' that is set up by the insurance company. They also will decide what codes they will pay and what conditions they will cover. In Florida, massage therapists can bill private health care insurance companies but they don't have to be providers. There are some states in which individual companies are 'willingly' paying for massage therapy services without the massage therapist having to be a contracted provider. While this section mainly applies to WA and FL, it can also help you learn what will happen in your state if and when massage becomes accepted by health insurance. It will also help you if you find an insurance company in your state that will pay for massage

To have your massage therapy services covered by an HMO or a PPO, you will need to become a provider with that organization and follow the rules of that insurance company or you will need to know which insurance companies will pay for massage. Most states do not recognize massage therapists as providers so the other option is to just call each company to find out if they will pay for massage for whatever the condition is. You will have to find out which ones on a case by case basis and find other Massage therapists in your area to mentor you or share their information.

In general, you will need to know what to ask the client and the insurance company in order to be able to bill and get paid. The basic process will look something like this:

- Get the insurance information from the client – usually their policy Identification number, their name and date of birth.
- Call the insurance company and ask if they have massage therapy benefits.
- You will have to ask what is required in order to be able to get paid for massage therapy. Will you need a prescription? Will you need to work for a Chiropractor, MD or other provider? You may need to give them the CPT code that you will be billing for to see if they cover it. (More on CPT codes later.)

- You can ask how much they will pay per unit of the CPT code (a unit = 15 minutes so 4 units will make an hour.) Most do not cover hour and a half sessions but you can ask to see if they do.
- You will need to ask what you need to do to get paid – how and to whom to you send the bill? Do you need to send the prescription and chart notes? How long will it take to get paid? Can you bill electronically?

In WA State, massage therapists are allowed to be contracted providers with insurance companies. There is a credentialing process that the massage therapist has to go through. It starts with applying to each insurance company. Some companies are managed by other third party companies. The application process is intensive and will include things like your work history, if you have any claims against you and you may have to have proof of liability insurance. There are some companies who have closed their list to applicants and have not allowed massage therapists to become providers. There is one company that has been doing that for over 10 years.

The problem with being a contracted provider is that you don't have much say in what they pay you or much of anything. You are basically under their control.

Affinity Plans/Discount plans. There are some insurance companies that may ask you to become a provider and give their customers a discount on your services. These companies may ask you to pay a fee to join and make you provide a certain percentage discount of your fees. The idea is that they will give you clients through their membership directory and you give low cost massage. You will have to analyze for yourself to see if they are worth joining.

Self Insured Plans. Many large companies are able to secure their own form of insurance and may have one of the major carriers 'manage' their plan. This may include the Federal Government employees, unions, trusts and large corporations that can afford their own plans. Most often these plans do not cover massage. You will have to check to see if massage is covered or not.

Chapter Seven. Worker's Compensation or Labor and Industries.

Worker's compensation plans or Labor and Industries, policies and rules for billing vary for each state. This is the insurance you have if you get hurt at work in any way. If you are in a car accident at work, fall at work, get carpal tunnel syndrome from working or anything that is related to work, you will be covered through this insurance. As a therapist, wanting to provide services under worker compensation plans, requires that you become a provider for that state. Most states do allow massage therapists to bill for work related injuries but must check to be sure that is so in your state. The laws change quickly, so you will need to stay informed. You will need to contact the proper authority to see if they recognize massage therapy services. Some companies may also have their own type of worker's compensation plans. This is called being self-insured. The same rules usually apply but check to be sure. Find out what rules and regulations they have regarding massage therapy services.

Some questions to ask the department of labor or workers compensation board:

- Do I need to become a provider? If so what is the process?
- Do I need to work at a doctor's office? Does my work have to be supervised by a doctor?

- Do I need a referral/prescription to work on patients?
- Do I need an authorization code? Do I need authorization?
- What CPT™ codes can I bill for? How many units?
- How many sessions are allowed? Can this be renewed? What will be required for renewal?
- What is the process for billing? Is there a manual available?
- Do I need to send chart notes and the prescription with the bill?
- Is there a fee schedule?

Most labor boards have provider fee schedules and service manuals available so that you can learn how to bill them properly. You can find a list of the labor boards at http://www.workerscompensation.com/

Chapter Eight. CMS – 1500. The Billing Form Explained.

The CMS-1500 is a standard billing form that can be purchased at any office supply store. The CMS-1500 form is so named for its originator, the Centers for Medicare and Medicaid Services (CMS). Find out from each company that you plan to work with whether or not they will accept a copy or need a new form for each bill. If you are billing by hand this may provide a shortcut to billing. You can put all the patient information on the top half and make a copy of it. You can then just fill in the bottom with the dates of service etc. and save the time of writing out the full bill.

Some insurance companies will not allow hand written bills and require a new form for each client.

Here is one you can download from the CMS 1500 just to see what it looks like. http://www.nucc.org/images/stories/PDF/final_1500_claim_form.pdf

There are also companies like www.officeally.com that will allow you to enter client's data into a form and have the forms electronically submitted to the various insurance companies. The services are free for providers. They also provide practice management software that interacts with the billing software so you can just update your client records and then bill the insurance company directly.

Line by line instructions for filling out the CMS-1500 form:

Line 1. Type of insurance. Other (usually) for PI cases or workers compensation or Group Health Plan for health insurance

Line 1a. This is the ID number of the insured person, which is sometimes different from the client. It is usually the social security number, but that is now changing due to HIPAA requirements. It also could be a claim number in a MVA.

Line 2. Patient's name

Line 3. Patient's birth date: Male or Female

Line 4. Insured's name, Employer or whoever has the insurance policy , which may be different than the client: possibly a spouse or parent.

Line 5. Patient's address.

Line 6. Patient's relationship to insured.

Line 7. Insured's address : if same as patient put same.

Line 8. Patient's status

Line 9 –9d Other insurance- if they have a secondary insurance that may kick in later. This could be a regular health insurance policy that may be billed for a MVA after funds are depleted or some other secondary insurance.

Line 10. What is patient's condition related to? Employment, auto accident or other. If you are billing a PPO for an Auto accident, be sure to check appropriate box.

Line 11a. Insured's Policy Number or Claim Number.

Line 11b. Employer or School

Line 11c. Insurance Plan name or program

Line 12, 13. Have the client sign a release of records statement on their intake form and keep the form on file. Fill this in with "on file". There may be states where you can't do this.

Line 14. Date of Injury or accident

Line 15. If applicable

Line 16. Provided by doctor

Line 17. Name of referring physician

Line 17a. ID number of referring physician (usually not needed)
Line 17b . NPI number of physician. You can look up the number at the National Plan and Provider Enumeration System (**NPPES**)

(https://nppes.cms.hhs.gov/NPPES/Welcome.do) (Some insurance companies may require this but others won't.)

Line 18. Leave blank

Line 19. Leave blank

Line 20. Leave blank

Line 21. Diagnosis Code. ICD-9 code. YOU MUST HAVE THIS! **This number is provided by the physician.** Even if they just put back pain, make the doctors give you the diagnosis code, even if you know what the code for back pain is.

Line 22. Leave Blank

Line 23. Leave blank or put referral number from HMO or PPO.

Line 24A. Dates of Service- one date per line. From and to are the same date.

Line 24B. Place of Service. Ask the insurance company what you should use there. It varies what codes they use. Every billing manual I have read says something different. It is usually a 3, 11 or OF. Ask the insurance company.

1. Inpatient hospital
2. Outpatient hospital
3. Office

4. Residence

5. Emergency Room

6. Other Medical/Surgical Facilities

7. Nursing homes

8. Other location

11. Office

12. Home

21. Hospital

22. outpatient hospital

34. Hospice

Line 24C. Type of Service. Ask the insurance company what you should use. It is usually a 9 for ancillary services.

Line 24D. CPT code goes here. Make sure you use the right CPT code for the procedure you are performing. Some companies will only pay for certain codes. See more on codes.
Line 24E. Diagnosis Code – Indicate which code from line 21 you are treating for.
Line 23F. Charges for Service- Total Charges

Line 24G. Days or Units – codes are usually designating 15 minutes of treatment so one hour would be 4 units.

Line 24 H. Leave Blank

Line 24 I. Leave Blank

Line 24 J . Your NPI number. Get one from the National Plan and Provider Enumeration System **(NPPES)**

Line 25. Your federal ID Number or SS#.

Line 26. Your patients account number: optional
Line 27. Leave Blank

Line 28. Total Charges for all days

Line 29. Enter amount of co-pay or other payment or leave blank

Line 30. Balance Due

Line 31. Your signature

Line 32. Leave blank unless you provided service somewhere else besides your office which may or may not be legal.

Line 33. Your name, address, provider number

33a. Your NPI number

33 b. Other provider number (if you have one from insurance company.) For more instructions see the official instruction sheet from www.nucc.org

Chapter Nine. CPT Codes and ICD-9 Codes.

CPT codes or Current Procedural Techniques codes and ICD-9 or International Classification of Disease codes (9th edition) are determined by the American Medical Association (AMA). New codes are created every 10 years. They will make the difference in how, when and what you will be paid. ICD-10 codes are in the works and are to be implemented by Oct 1, 2013 with Jan. 2012 as the starting date for rolling out the new codes. Here is some info on the dates and transitions from the CMS. (https://www.cms.gov/ICD10/)

The most common codes used by massage therapists are codes that are used by physical therapists as the massage profession does not have their own category (yet!). There really are no regulations as to who can use the codes as long as the health care provider is properly trained and licensed. (A physician can do massage and bill 97124 as long as they have training in massage). If another health care practitioner bills for the same code on the same date, you may not be paid (concurrent care). (If a chiropractor sees the patient on the same day as you and bills for 1 unit of 97124 and you bill 4 units of 97124, you will not be paid for 1 unit if that goes over the allowable number of units.)

You have to determine which code is applicable to the type of massage work you do. Some companies will pay more for one code but you cannot use that code unless you are actually doing that type of massage.

97124 - Therapeutic procedure, one or more areas, each 15 minutes: massage including effleruage, petrissage and/or tapotement (stroking, compression, percussion; therapeutic massage.

97140 - Manual Therapy techniques: mobilization, manipulation, manual lymphatic drainage, manual traction, one or more regions, each 15 minutes.

97122 - Therapeutic procedure, one or more areas, each 15 minutes: Neuromuscular re-education of movement, balance, coordination, kinesthetic sense, posture and proprioception. (this would include Proprioceptive Neuromuscular Facilitation (PNF), Feldenkrais but not St. John's Neuromuscular Therapy.)

97010 – Hot/cold packs

Some miscellaneous codes that are often questionable at this time are because they are out of the scope of practice of massage therapists :

97018 – paraffin bath

97022- whirlpool

97026 -infrared

97122- traction, manual

97530- therapeutic activities, each 15 minutes

97110- therapeutic exercise, each 15 minutes

It is your responsibility to choose the code that best fits your work. Some companies will also only pay for one of the codes, while some may pay for many of the other codes. For example: one insurance company I work with will only pay for the code 97124 and not 97140, while another company recognizes both.

The ICD-9 (International Classification of Disease):

The ICD-9 Code **must be** supplied by the referring physician as massage therapists are not allowed to diagnose any conditions. There are many different codes to describe different conditions and diseases. It is important to get the correct code. There are a few insurance companies that will not require a prescription from a doctor yet will require that a code be placed in the diagnosis code section in order to get paid. Diana Thompson, author of "Hands Heal" advises that you are able to use a general pain code as it is not a diagnosis but a description of the pain.

There is a Code chart in the appendix for reference for when the doctor just writes the code down on the prescription but not what it is.

You can also look up the codes online when you use www.officeally.com or use one of the free services like http://www.medilexicon.com/icd9codes.php or

http://icd9cm.chrisendres.com/index.php

Codes will change in Oct. 2013 to the ICD-10 format.

Chapter Ten. Documentation. SOAP Notes, Progress Reports, Narrative Reports.

Your chart notes are the most important part of getting paid for your services. Keep in mind that the work you do with a client will be scrutinized, reviewed and even judged for medical necessity in a court of law. The main purpose of chart notes is to show progress in a patients/clients condition and functioning. Just charting pain and pain levels is not really showing progress or improvement of functioning.

I could write a complete book on the topic, but there is already a good one out there. "Hands Heal: Communication, Documentation, and Insurance Billing for Manual Therapists" by Diana L. Thompson, is a complete guide to charting.

The key to getting paid by insurance companies is proving that the massage that you are doing is "medically necessary". (Each insurance company and each insurance plan, has their own definition of medical necessity. You will need to know what it is. You can ask or look on some of their websites.)

We do that through the use of chart notes. There are many ways of taking chart notes. The most common are "SOAP" (**S**ubjective, **O**bjective, **A**ssessment, **P**lan) notes. To prove medical necessity, we must show that the client's condition has improved as a result of massage. While some people have said that medical necessity is the responsibility of the referring physician, here in WA State we are asked to provide chart notes to the insurance companies to prove medical necessity. Some companies will require that you send chart notes with the bill before they will send payment. Call the insurance company first to find out before sending the bill.

Using SOAP charts is the most effective way to communicate what you do in a session. This can help get massage more accepted by insurance companies and by the medical profession in general. The purpose of SOAP charts are to record the clients' condition and the progress that occurs in each session of bodywork/massage. It is usually required for sessions that will be paid for by an insurance company, whether it is a PIP (auto insurance), L&I (Labor and Industries) or Major Medical. Your records may be requested by physicians to keep them updated on the condition of the client or by lawyers who need them as records of the clients' injury and progress. Either way, it is important to keep the clients charts updated and complete. See also an alternative to SOAP notes – CARE Notes
http://www.massageandbodywork.com/Articles/AprilMay2003/CAREnotes.html)

Subjective: This means subjective complaints and symptoms in the client's own words or perhaps what was said (as recounted to you) by the prescribing physician. This includes all the things the client tells you about how they are feeling, past history, present symptoms, limitations in their lives due to the injury, what makes them feel better or worse, and details about the ini- tial onset of the problem or injury. It is often helpful to ask the client to rate their pain or discomfort on a level 1-10 with 10 being the worst. If you do this each time, you will be able to see improvements or setbacks. Tracking pain levels though, do not always show or clearly show progress. More specifically, track the changes in the patients function in activities such as walking, sitting, sleeping or driving. How long can they sit, stand or function and what limits their ability to do those things. Tracking functional outcomes is the core of SOAP charting and you can get the full details on how to do that in Diana Thompson's book : Hands Heal: Communication, Documentation, and Insurance Billing for Manual Therapists

Ask specific questions as to the location, intensity, duration and frequency of the pain or discomfort. Have the client point to the specific area on their body or body chart. Ask how painful is it? How long have they had it? Hours? Weeks? Months? Longer? Has it been worse or better? What makes it worse or better? How often do they get it? Every day? Once a week?

Asking specific questions will lead to a clearer picture of the problem/injury you are treating.

Objective: These are the observations of the practitioner along with the techniques used in the session. This includes visual observations and what you feel in the body of the client. Include things you observe about the client's posture, patterns, movement, weakness, level of tension in the tissues, spasms in muscles, joint movement, color/temperature of skin and breathing patterns.

You can also test the range of motion in different areas and keep track of their improvement or changing patterns.

Some common findings are defined below:

Hypertonicity: involuntarily tight or contracted muscle; excess muscle tone; the tension of the resting muscle is unusually high.

Spasm: involuntary contraction of a muscle as a protective response to an injury or trauma.

Trigger point: specific point that refers pain

Adhesion/scar tissue: the resulting tissue from the wound healing process causing a restriction in resiliency of the tissue

Measure everything! That way you can show improvement to illustrate medical necessity.

Assessment: Assessment usually involves collecting the information from the subjective and objective part to make a diagnosis or prognosis on the clients' condition. Since massage therapists are not allowed to diagnose, the assessment is to report the changes that occur in a session. This means to report the immediate results of the session (functional outcomes). At the end of the session reanalyze the posture and range of motion. Make notes on any changes in symptoms. Indicate how much change happened- mild, moderate or significant change. Use as many descriptive words as possible.

Most insurance companies will take this information into consideration when paying for the treatment. This tells them if the client is getting better and helps them decide whether the treatment is worth the cost. Here, you can include the doctor's diagnosis.

Plan: Suggest a treatment frequency and items that need to be addressed in the future. Include any self-care instructions you gave to the client, special requests by the client, or reminders for the next session. You can include your goals for the client- what results do you expect or what you think the outcome will be. The physician usually provides treatment plans that include how many sessions and how often sessions are to be given and what areas are to be worked on.

Insurance companies need to see improvement in a client to verify "medical necessity". One method of showing this is to include "functional outcomes" in your SOAP notes. Functional outcomes are the improvements in function that occur as a result of your massage. To chart functional outcomes you must first find out what functions are limited. Start with the basics like walking, turning their head, sitting, or standing. Do they have functional limits due to their condition? You can then chart the progress of how their function has improved as a result of the massage. Insurance companies don't care about pain levels, hypertonicities and spasms. They often assume that the client will have to live with a certain amount of pain. This is one of my professional concerns. Do we as a profession even want to be dealing with such companies? Decreasing pain, does not necessarily mean progress according to insurance companies. (For a full explanation of functional outcomes see Hands Heal: Communication, Documentation, and Insurance Billing for Manual Therapists" by Diana L. Thompson)

Progress Reports:

Physicians may request progress reports to keep them informed as to progress. It is a good idea to call the physician and ask if they want/require progress reports. Progress reports are also used to ask for a prescription renewal.

Sending the progress notes is a great way to build a working relationship with a physician or other health care professional.

With HIPAA rules and regulations, you will need to have the client sign a release of records that will allow you to communicate with the physician about their case.

A progress report can be a simple chart that outlines what improvement has been made in the client's condition. (See sample in appendix)

Narrative Report

Narrative Reports are usually requested by attorneys to summarize the client's injuries, treatments and progress. They use these reports to prove to the insurance company just how badly the person was injured. They will use the reports to try and determine the amount of settlement due to the client. It is usually in letter form and contains a generalization of what treatment has been done to resolve the client's injuries.

It is necessary to keep accurate chart notes so that you can write a narrative report.

You can ask the attorney what details they want in the report. (See also: Hands Heal: Communication, Documentation, and Insurance Billing for Manual Therapists" by Diana L. Thompson)

Chapter Eleven. Getting Paid and What to do if You Don't Get Paid.

Getting paid is the challenge. Insurance companies will deny payments for varying reasons You will have to decide if the reason for denial can be appealed and how much time you want to put into the appeal process. Here are some of the reasons which can be corrected or challenged:

- Incorrect procedure or diagnosis codes
- Incomplete form: no diagnosis code, claim numbers etc.
- Lost bills
- Missing physician's referral or prescription
- Outdated referral or prescription
- Treating other areas not included in the diagnosis code
- Palliative care
- Higher than usual UCR fees.
- Didn't send a copy of the prescription or referral with the bill (not all require this)
- The data entry person was having a bad day
- The insurance company wanted to keep the money for themselves for a while longer.

- Some insurance companies may only allow so many dates of service per bill (I haven't had this problem – but have heard of others having it)
- No prior authorization for treatment
- No progress notes or chart notes sent with the bill

When a bill is denied, the insurance company is responsible for letting you know why it has been denied. It often is denied for an incomplete form, but there are also many other reasons.

The key to getting paid is finding out ahead of time what each insurance company requires when you send the bill. Start with the questions in the last chapter. If you are a provider with a company, they will usually have a manual with all the instructions. It is recommended that you call each company as you acquire new clients and speak with a representative about what they want and what massage therapy benefits they allow. You may have to find the right person to talk to. It often is the case manager, the actual billing person or it could be a provider representative. It helps to call a few times and ask the same questions to different people. You will find differences in what the service representative will tell you. This will give you an idea of what it will be like working with this company. If the client has an attorney, you should call and ask the attorney the same questions. See what they require from you before you get too involved in the case. It is good to get acquainted and set up a good working relationship with the legal representatives as you will probably work together in other cases.

I have often had insurance com- panies tell me that a prescription or referral is not needed and when my bill is rejected it is denied due to lack of diagnosis code. This code must come from the physician, <u>massage therapists are not allowed to diagnose</u>. The confusion is that some plans say that they don't require a referral but they don't specify that it does not include massage therapists.

If you don't get paid, you will have some work to do. When you call insurance companies it is very important to keep track of who you talked to, what they said and what they said they would do. Insurance companies often record their phone calls. I once got an insurance company to pay based on what was said in a recorded phone call. But that means you must take notes while you are talking to the company.

When you bill insurance companies, you will just have to accept the fact that there will be problems and it will take time to get paid. The people who work for insurance companies are not the ones to blame for not getting paid. It is important to start out with respect and courtesy when working with any representative. You will find that people will go out of their way to help you. But, when you find you have run out of options for getting the situation resolved, you may need to speak to a supervisor. The problem that you will face is that the supervisor may not be informed of your case, so it is important to keep good notes on what you have done to try and resolve the situation.

It is also important to get the client involved in such a situation. After all, they will be the one who is responsible for paying the bill if the insurance company fails to pay. Give them the tracking form to help track the calls. Letting the client take responsibility for collecting payment takes the burden off of you.

When all else fails you can ask the client to file a complaint with the insurance commissioner's office. Providers generally can't file complaints, but may be able to write a letter that the client can provide as evidence that payment is due.

Chapter Twelve. Networking to Build Your Practice.

One of the best ways to build your business is by networking with Physicians, Naturopaths, Acupuncturists and other medical providers.

Once you get a referral from a health care provider, make sure you take advantage of the opportunity to network with that provider. You can do this in a few different ways.

- Send a thank you for the referral letter/postcard (but don't use the client's name because of HIPAA.)
- Send an initial evaluation report after the first appointment.
- Send a progress report whether they request one or not.
- Send a letter to thank them along with a brochure, business cards and/or a specific referral form.
- Most providers will benefit from getting more information about what kinds of conditions and problems that you work with. Most don't realize what massage can be used for. Educating them should be included in your marketing plan.
- Build a website so you can provide more information to the providers about yourself and your business. You can learn more about building a website at www.massagepracticebuilder.com

One of best ways to build referral network is to pick out a few doctors or other health care providers that you truly respect. Who would you go to if you were sick or injured? Who would you send one of your clients or family members to, for treatment? Working with someone who you respect is the basis for building a solid relationship. I believe it takes a team of health care practitioners to support clients who are injured or ill. It is necessary to address all aspects of the mind, body and spirit for healing. Working with a team of Naturopaths, doctors, chiropractors, acupuncturists, physical therapists and psychologists who can all work together and who understand each others work is essential.

I am amazed at the number of massage therapists who accept referrals from chiropractors and they have never been to a chiropractor, nor do they really understand what they do. It is also important to respect that type of treatment. If you won't go to a chiropractor yourself, why would you want to work on someone who is seeing one? It will usually cause conflicts in treatments if you start working with someone who you don't respect or who you won't go to yourself for care. Learning about the other providers' theories on healing, tools and techniques can further support the client. Learn to talk to doctors in their own language using medical terms but make sure you know what you are talking about.

Once you pick out a few good practitioners in your area, start contacting them either by phone, email or letter. The best way to contact them is to ask about them and what they do first. Show that you are interested in learning about them, so that you can refer clients to them first. Asking about the type of work they do allows them to feel like they are accepted and needed. It opens up the doors for them to be receptive of what you have to offer.

You can also start by asking the health care providers that you do go to for referrals. I went to a chiropractor when I first started out who started referring people to me. I didn't even really ask. Building a network is not totally about building your practice – it is about being of service to the client. Your practice will grow when you act with integrity to build it. If your first concern is to only work with others that you trust and respect, your clients will have more respect for you.

One of the things that doctors understand and respect is research. As a massage therapist, you must understand how to read and interpret research material and learn how to use it when talking with doctors and clients/patients. The Massage Therapy Foundation and the Touch Research Institute have many resources listing the latest massage research. One of the ways to use this resource is to actually go and start collecting research on a specific condition that is really common like back pain or fibromyalgia or depression/anxiety disorders. You can become the expert on what the research says in those areas and create a special report to send to doctors and can also put that information on your website for everyone to see. You can also put it in a special 'Doctors Only' section on your website if you like.

Sample Networking Letter

My Massage Practice

2012 Billing Lane Dr

Yahoo I am Rich, WA 10000-0000

January 1 2012

Dr. Caring World

2222 Success Lane

Plentyful, WA 10000

Dear Dr. World.
I am writing to introduce myself and my massage business to you and hope to develop a working alliance with you. I have had many clients who are your patients who have informed me that you see many patients that have work related injuries like carpal tunnel syndrome. I was just writing to let you know that I specialize in just those type of injuries, specifically carpal tunnel syndrome. I often refer people out to specialists and thought that we might be a good match for working together with this challenging condition.

There is current research that shows that massage can help reduce and eliminate the symptoms of carpal tunnel syndrome. [Carpal tunnel syndrome symptoms are lessened following massage therapy Tiffany Field, Miguel Diego, Christy Cullen, Kristin Hartshorn, Alan Gruskin, Maria Hernandez-Reif, William SunshineTouch Research Institutes,

University of Miami School of Medicine, PO Box 016820 (D-820), Miami, FL 33101]

I use triggerpoint therapy to release the trigger points and tightness in the forearms, arms, shoulders and neck to get people back doing what they love most. Most see results with a series of weekly or twice a week sessions depending on the severity of the case.

Massage Therapy as you may know is also covered by insurance here in WA so a prescription is needed that contains a treatment plan as well as the diagnosis. I can also send progress reports as needed. I look forward to working with you. Let me know if you have any questions.

I can send referral pads for your convenience. You can order them at any time through my website and learn more about my credentials and skills there to. www.carpaltunnelmassageportland.com

Thank You.

Worlds' Best Massage Therapist.

Chapter Thirteen. Putting It All Together.

So now with all this information, how do you find out what to do in your state and what insurance companies will pay you? You just need to start asking questions. It is all about learning what questions to ask and who has the answers you need. It will take a little bit of learning and trial and error, until you find your way and learn what cases to take and which to not take. This is where another big challenge comes in as far as creating boundaries that support your massage business. You may be forced to say No to a regular client or risk having more headaches and financial difficulties.

You will need to call prospective insurance companies to find out what you need to do. You will need to talk to lawyers. You will need to talk to clients. There is a list of them at your State Insurance Commissioners office website. You can also wait and do this when a client asks you to bill their insurance company.

Screening Clients when they call:

- Ask what type of injury they have. See if it is something that you want to work with or can work with.
- Were they injured in a motor vehicle collision, hurt at work or in an accident at work? If they are hurt at work,

you will need to be bill the Workers Compensation or Labor and Industries. If hurt in a car accident, you will be billing the car insurance.

- If it is a work related injury, you need to know what rules apply to billing Workers Compensation or Labor and Industries in your state.
- If it is a car accident, find out what kind of insurance they have and find out what coverage they have. You may have to get their insurance information and call the insurance company or ask them to call first to get the details. You can use the insurance verification form in the appendix. It is always a good idea to call yourself and speak with the adjuster to see how they want bills sent.
- If it is a private health insurance, you will have to find out if they will pay for massage. WA and FL are the only two states that currently allow this, but more companies are willingly paying. You will have to call them one by one or talk to other Massage Therapists in your area to find out who is paying.
- Have the client/patient call their insurance to verify benefits and fill out a verification form to make your work easier or to confirm your findings.
- When they come in, the client/patient must fill out the appropriate forms: Intake, HIPAA forms, informed consent if applicable.

- If hurt in a car accident or at work, do they have an attorney?
- If it is a car accident, you will need to know if there is PIP or Med Pay coverage that will pay you up front. Otherwise, you will be waiting until settlement for payment which could be 1-3 years or even more depending on the laws in your state.
- Decide if you need to file a lien to secure payment.

How to get paid –Calling the insurance company to Verify Benefits and Billing Procedures

Here is a checklist of questions you will need to ask each company:

- Do you pay for massage therapy services?
- Are massage therapy services covered by this client's policy?
- What rules are there for billing, as in some plans require that you work for a chiropractor or other healthcare provider.
- Do I need to be on a provider list? If so what is the process for becoming a provider? (Most worker's compensation or Labor and Industries systems require that you apply.)
- What CPT codes do you allow for massage therapy services? (Some companies only allow certain codes to be billed by massage therapists.) How many units of each code are allowed? (4 units = 1 hour: can you bill for more than an hour? – usually not, but in some cases you can). You can also tell them what code you bill and ask if they will allow this code and what is the allowable fee (what will they pay).

- Can I bill multiple codes? What other codes?
- What combination of codes can I bill? Tell them what codes you use and find out if they will pay you for those codes.
- What is the allowable fee per code? This is the amount they will pay. Some insurance companies do not pay enough to make the whole process worth it all.
- Do I need a prescription from the physician? (If they say no, it is always a good idea to get one anyway.) If they say no, ask if a Diagnosis code (ICD-9) code is necessary. If so, then point out that a prescription will be necessary, as you are not allowed to make a diagnosis.
- Do I need a referral? A referral may be different than a prescription. It may involve the physician initiating the referral to the insurance company and they send the referral to you.
- Is there any restriction on the Diagnosis code? Can you treat for all codes or will there be some that won't be allowed? Tell them the diagnosis code that the doctor provided to see if it is covered.
- Do I need to send chart notes when submitting a bill?
- Do I need to send the prescription when submitting a bill?
- What is the normal processing time for payments?
- Where do I send the bill? Do I need to send it to anyone's attention? Can I/ should I bill electronically?
- Is there any statue of limitations on the time allowed to bill for services? If there are any problems with the bill and it is rejected, how much time do you have to resubmit it. Most companies allow 6 months to a year. After that time, you will not be paid no

matter what. In some cases, it may take that amount of time to get the bill straightened out.

- What are the policy limits and benefits? Some policies have a dollar limit or number of treatment limit or a time limit like 3 years.
- How much of the available funds/sessions have been used? Has the client had previous treatment from another massage therapist that used some of the allowable benefits?
- Is there a deductible? Has it been met?
- Is there a co-insurance or co-pay?
- Do I need to submit a W-2 form? This is often needed, as companies will supply you with a 1099 form for tax purposes.

Even after everything is verified and approved on the phone or through whatever communication, you still may not be paid or paid in full for your massage services. Verification does not automatically mean a guarantee of payment.

You can also put this all in the hands of the client and get them involved in the process.

The other things that can save you time are:

- Have the client call and verify benefits using the form in the appendix.
- Send bills registered or certified mail to ensure their delivery, or bill electronically.

- Double check the billing form to make sure it is filled out completely. Make sure all information is correct.
- Don't work without a prescription. The prescription should include the diagnosis, treatment plan and usually starts on the day they sign it.

It is often difficult to find the right person to talk to at an insurance company. Most companies have a customer service representative for your area. Be persistent if you are not getting your questions answered. Other people that may be of help to you are the billing specialist (the person who actually keys the bill into the computer), the claims adjuster, the case manager, and the lawyer or paralegal.

When the client arrives:

- Create a file for each client and have a secure place for keeping files.
- They should have the insurance verification form filled out.
- Fill out an intake form and do a thorough intake interview
- Make a copy of the insurance card or claim card.
- Get the prescription from the patient that documents the diagnosis and specific treatment plan and keep it in the file and keep it updated and current.
- Provide the billing contact information and attorney if applicable.
- Sign HIPAA Forms

- Sign a Lien Form if applicable.
- Contact the insurance company and the attorney if they have one.
- Complete SOAP notes on each client.
- Send the bill ASAP.
- Track bills and payments with the form in the appendix.
- Follow up with the bill if payment has not been received.

Often you will not be able to get all of your questions answered! The key to getting paid is to accept the fact that you will have problems getting paid and will have problems working with insurance companies! But that persistence pays off.

Chapter Fourteen. The Challenges of Billing.

Billing insurance has been such a mixed blessing for my massage practice. On one hand it has allowed me to keep a business going for over 23 years. On the other hand it has been one of the biggest challenges as working with the insurance companies and doctors is very challenging from the aspect of what has to be done to get paid and has taught me more about boundaries and ethics than most any other aspect of running a massage business.

It is a mixed blessing that more and more insurance companies are allowing massage therapists to become providers and are paying for massage therapy services. On one hand we are being recognized as health care providers. On the other hand our work is being limited and controlled by big insurance companies that focus on the bottom line of making money. They tell us how long our sessions should be, how often we can see the client, for what duration, for what conditions and how we should be treating them. Many massage therapists want to avoid taking insurance and being a player in the game which is totally understandable.

There are a lot of people who will not go for massage because it is not covered in their policy. Some will only go for the allotted number of treatments and stop after that. This is usually a result of people not understanding what massage can do. Educating people to take responsibility for their health and well-being is essential. It is not just about "fixing" that shoulder problem or back problem.

I also believe that there is much more to healing than "fixing" clients symptoms. Healing requires teams of support so that the client can look at the deeper issues of what may be causing them to overwork, not take care of themselves and end up sick or injured. We all know that there is much more to musculo-skeletal pain than meets the eye. Repressed emotions and spiritual conflicts may often be the cause of pain. We build up physical armor to protect ourselves from the stress around us and in us.

Being a part of networks and billing insurance companies that are based on the medical model of healing pain, really limit healing and the ability of the client to find their wholeness. The current medical model takes us away from being of service and forces us to "fix". It challenges what we do as massage therapists. I have so many clients who come in with some sort of pain and leave saying that their relationships are better, their work life is better or they are making major changes to their life to be more in tune with their values. How can we enter into the system and maintain the healing qualities and art of massage? It is done through the process of supervision and being able to talk about the challenges of working with insurance companies. The way out of "caretaking" and "fixing" and being a slave to insurance companies is through supervision. Supervision is not really what you may think of when you hear that word -as in a supervisor at work – IT IS NOT THAT! Supervision is the process of working with a more experienced massage therapist for the purpose of talking about and understanding all of your ethical concerns, learning to set and enforce boundaries and to provide a safe place for massage therapists to deal with the daily issues of being a massage therapist. One of the main reasons for supervision is to take a look at who's needs are being met in a session – the clients or the massage therapists. The more we can focus on the client and get our own needs met outside of a massage business, the better your chances for success as a massage therapist. Building community peer supervision groups and seeking out individual supervisors where we can share our stories and come to know our stories better, are the key to being able to work with insurance companies without losing track of the real massage. You can find out more about supervision at www.massagepracticebuilder.com

Other challenges that you will find is that in general, when clients do not pay cash for their sessions and let the insurance pay, it seems like they are susceptible to thinking that their health is out of their hands and solely rests in your hands. I have found through the years that many people who come in and are having their insurance pay don't take their care as seriously and are sometimes the first to cancel at the last minute or not show up for their appointments. (Oh and by the way, you can not bill the insurance for a missed appointment. It is up to you to create and enforce a cancellation policy for your insurance clients.) I am not saying that all people who are injured and seeking massage are like that, but it is just something that seems to occur. People who are paying cash are more invested in their healing and respect your time more.

I have already talked about the challenge of setting your fees for massage services in the second chapter. This is another big dilemma for many massage therapists as they automatically see dollar signs when thinking about billing for massage. Yes it is true, you can make a little more per hour and have a steady flow of clients in any economy. Setting your fees so that they are in alignment with your values and beliefs is an important part of being successful. Creating and enforcing a cancellation policy and no show policy goes right along with the money issues. Since insurance does not pay for no shows or missed appointments, you will have to charge the client directly for the time. That can be difficult especially in cases with severely injured patients/clients who may be out of work or faced with very large medical bills due to their condition.

Working for a chiropractor or other health care professional as an independent contractor can be a sticky situation especially if you pay them a percentage of your income because of kickback laws that might be in effect in your state. You will have to find out what the law is and set up your IC status accordingly.

Some chiropractors or other health care professionals may also be over-billing for massage and paying the massage therapist a low or reasonable wage. I have seen instances of chiropractors billing in excess of $200 for a one hour massage session which is really very questionable. If you find yourself working for someone like this, it will of course be a difficult situation. If you bring it up or challenge them, you could lose your job. If you don't, you may feel like you are part of the problem of over-billing.

The answer to all of these situations can be found in participating in regular individual supervision with a more experienced massage therapists or counselor, meeting regularly with a group of peers specifically for this purpose.

It is also possible to build and maintain a practice that is 100% cash and forget this whole insurance stuff and also be successful!

Chapter Fifteen. Getting More Health Insurance to Pay.

In WA State, we are contracted providers with private health insurance companies such as Aetna, Premera Blue Cross and Regence Blue Shield.

Becoming a Preferred Provider:

Washington State allows massage therapists to become providers. We have a law that was enacted by the insurance commissioner, Deborah Senn in 1996 called the "every category law". It requires all insurance companies to allow massage therapists to become providers and requires insurance companies to pay for our services. Companies fought this at first, but it was overturned and is now constantly being challenged each year. I did talk to Deborah Senn about whether or not this can be done in other states and she replied a firm "Yes." All states can have a law like this created that will mandate that Massage therapists must be able to become a contracted provider or be paid by the insurance companies. What it takes is someone standing up for the profession like Deborah Senn did. The rules and regulations vary from state to state and each company has various plans. In general, most require that you have a referral/prescription from the Primary Care Physician (PCP) since massage therapists are not allowed to diagnose conditions. You will find that massage will only be covered when used for rehabilitative purposes (when there is an injury or health problem). Relaxation /wellness massage not covered at this time.

One of the big things that Deborah Senn mentioned in her talk at the Massage Research Conference was the fact that the insurance companies did not understand how massage would work. They thought that they would have to be paying the Orthopedic Surgeon their fees for surgery (say $10,000) and then an additional fee for the massage therapist (say $1000) for something like carpal tunnel syndrome. They do not understand that it could possibly eliminate the surgeon's and hospital bills and the time off from work for the patient. This should be the focus of any campaign to get massage be more accepted. Show the insurance companies how massage can save them money. I have also heard of some massage therapists actually doing this case by case and showing the insurance companies that massage would save them money. It takes more time and energy to do that, but it is teaching the insurance companies how massage works.

There are a few things to consider when thinking about joining a PPO or HMO:

- You usually will not be reimbursed for your full fees. The insurance company determines what they will allow for massage therapy services. When you are under contract with such an organization, you are not allowed to bill the difference to the client. The PPO can change what they pay at any time and you must accept that as final payment.

- Each year they have reduced the amount that they will allow and have made it more difficult to get paid. They also have decreased policy benefits for massage therapy services.
- The insurance company determines which codes and services you may provide. For example: The PPO I belong to at first allowed me to bill for using hydrotherapy (ice or heat packs) and would allow me to bill for this service separately. They decided to not allow this service. Since I signed the contract with them, I have no alternatives but to go along with what they decide about reimbursement. Does these mean I should not use ice or heat packs even though I think they will be beneficial? This is the type of professional ethical issue that you will be faced with.
- Your work hours will be increased with the amount of paperwork and phone calls you need to make to collect on the bills. You will often get insurance companies denying payment if you fill out the form incorrectly.

On the other hand becoming a member in such an organization will bring you a continual stream of clients. What you are getting in return for accepting a reduced rate for your services is marketing for your business. You will get a listing in their provider directory. Potential clients will often seek you out because you are close to their work or home and it will be easy to get to your office. You may be working more, but it may be for less money. Although this may assist you in building your practice, it is not advised to base your practice solely on insurance income.

Here in Washington State, most insurance company providers lists are closed as they claim to have too many massage therapy providers.

Suggestions on How to become a provider

1. Find out who your insurance commissioner is.
2. Start a campaign to educate them as to the benefits of massage.
3. Start a letter writing campaign to start telling them about the latest research on how massage can help. Focus on the amount of money massage can SAVE them. The insurance companies in WA at first thought that massage was going to be in addition to the amount that they were already paying out in doctors fees. They did not realize that they would be able to save money on patient's treatments and avoid surgeries.
4. Provide massage to legislators.
5. Get more support from massage organization such as AMTA and ABMP to hire attorneys to read contracts and help stand up for massage therapists.

The Affordable Care Act passed by President Obama in 2010 does have a new section that looks like it will make it so that all massage therapists in every state will be able to bill insurance. It goes into effect in Jan 2014. It is pretty much like the WA State Every Category Law. It states:

> *(Section 2706) "A group health plan and a health insurance issuer offering group or individual health insurance coverage shall not discriminate with respect to participation under the plan or coverage against any health care provider who is acting within the scope of that provider's license or certification under applicable State law."*

So you might want to see how the election goes and if the Health Care Reform Act stays in effect but you will still have to get it implemented by the insurance commissioner. When WA State started out, there was a big report done called "Issues in Coverage for Complementary and Alternative Medicine Services" that you can read part of online at http://www.docstoc.com/docs/28819614/ISSUES-IN-COVERAGE-FOR-COMPLEMENTARY-AND-ALTERNATIVE-MEDICINE. It was done in 2000 so some information needs to be updated but it will give you some ideas on what is needed and what was done here in WA State.

Currently, more insurance companies are willingly paying for massage services. There are even some companies who have added Complementary and Alternative Medicine Plans to their list of employee benefits. You will have to call one by one or connect with another massage therapist in your area that is currently billing companies and find out what companies are paying.

There are incidences of massage therapists also taking the time to show the insurance company just how much money that massage can save them by carefully documenting their sessions for conditions like carpal tunnel syndrome or other things that usually require surgery and showing the insurance company that by getting massage, it can help reduce and eliminate various conditions without having to have costly surgery. Insurance companies are always looking for the best use of their money to cut costs. You can also supplement your case with research that shows what massage can do.

Chapter Sixteen. Hiring a Billing Person.

If after reading this manual and billing a few cases you decide that you would rather spend your time doing massage and hire a person to bill the insurance here are some tips on how to do that.

- When you hire someone to bill for you and you are billing electronically, you will have to inform people how you are sharing their info through a billing person. You will also have to set up a safe way to transfer information to the billing person.
- They must be able to implement all of the steps in this book and have a tracking system to follow up with the billing.
- You will have to keep on top of the actions of your billing person, making sure that they are doing the billing within the allotted time frames and submitting the bills in a timely manner.
- They must be knowledgeable of billing and billing procedures.

Hiring someone to do the billing, paperwork and keep up with the laws and procedures for billing can let you do what you do best – Massage!

Chapter Seventeen. Glossary.

Advocacy- Any activity done to help a person or group to get something the person or group needs or wants.

Adjuster – The insurance representative assigned to the client's case that reviews and authorizes or denies payment. The adjuster is also known as the claim manager. Not all companies have assigned adjusters. Claims are usually sent to the adjuster in a personal injury case. You may have to get authorization from the adjuster to begin treatment.

Affidavit – A written statement made under oath. You may be asked to make or sign an affidavit that describes the treatment and condition of the client. Accurate chart notes are necessary to make statements to be used in an affidavit.

Affinity Plan or Network – A type of insurance contract that requires providers to offer their services at a discounted fee.

Allowable Fee – The maximum amount that each insurance company will pay. This is usually based on the Usual, Customary and Reasonable Fee (UCR), but not always. They will only pay this amount no matter what you charge. If you are contracted with a provider network, you are may be unable to charge the difference to your client.

Ancillary- That which assists or supports the primary treatment or a service; supplemental

Arbitration – An alternative to going to court for dispute resolution. Clients who are seeking a settlement from an insurance company and don't want to go to court can pay for arbitration services. The third party (arbitrator) reviews the case and imposes a decision that is legally binding for both sides. Arbitrators are usually lawyers or retired judges but can also be other individuals with specialized training. The client and/or their attorney may ask you to appear to report your findings. You can charge the client for your appearance at the arbitration. Be prepared to speak about the clients' condition and how it has improved from your work and what is the client's current state of health in relation to their injuries. Having complete and in depth chart notes will help you in this process.

Assessment – The assessment (A) section of the SOAP chart records: the process of assessment involves interpreting the subjective and objective findings to make conclusions about the client's condition. Since we aren't allowed to diagnose, this is to report the immediate results of the session (functional outcomes).

Assignment of Benefits- Line 13 on the CMS 1500 form; When a client authorizes the provider to be paid directly for their services. You can have the client sign an assignment of benefit form.

Authorization – This is the pre-approval process to verify benefits and get approval from the insurance company (usually workers compensation or Labor and Industries) to treat the client. Even if you get a verbal authorization, it does not guarantee that you will be paid. It is advised that you start all claims by making a call to authorize or verify benefits. Clients will also have to authorize a release of records when insurance companies or attorneys request records to be sent.

Benefit - Amount payable by the insurance company to a claimant, assignee, or beneficiary when the insured suffers a loss.

Bodily Injury Insurance – Type of auto insurance that covers someone who is at-fault for bodily injuries that they have caused to others in an accident. It is paid in a lump sum for any future health care, pain and suffering, lost wages and permanent impairment or disability.

Bundling – Process of combining two or more health care procedures into one CPT code. I used to be able to charge for hot/cold packs, but they have now been bundled into the CPT code for therapeutic massage (97124).

Capitation- Capitation represents a set dollar limit that you or your employer pay to a health maintenance organization (HMO), regardless of how much you use (or don't use) the services offered by the health maintenance providers. (Providers is a term used for health professionals who provide care. Usually providers refer to doctors or hospitals. Sometimes the term also refers to nurse practitioners, chiropractors and other health professionals who offer specialized services.)

Carrier – The insurance company

Centers for Medicare & Medicaid Services (CMS) – was the HCFA or "**Health Care Financing Administration** is a federal agency within the United States Department of Health and Human Services (DHHS) that administers the Medicare program and works in partnership with state governments to administer Medicaid, the State Children's Health Insurance Program (SCHIP), and health insurance portability standards. In addition to these programs, CMS has other responsibilities, including the administrative simplification standards from the Health Insurance Portability and Accountability Act of 1996 (HIPAA), quality standards in long-term care facilities (more commonly referred to as nursing homes) through its survey and certification process, and clinical laboratory quality standards under the Clinical Laboratory Improvement Amendments."
http://en.wikipedia.org/wiki/Centers_for_Medicare_and_Medicaid_Services

Claim - A request by an individual (or his or her provider) to an individual's insurance company for the insurance company to pay for services obtained from a health care professional.

Clean Claim – A claim submitted to an insurance company that is complete and accurate. An insurance company won't pay the bill unless the claim is "clean". Some common errors include incorrect codes, incorrect patient information and anything else that the insurance company feels like at the time.

Co-Insurance- Co-insurance refers to money that an individual is required to pay for services, after a deductible has been paid. In some health care plans, co-insurance is called "co-payment." Co-insurance is often specified by a percentage. For example, the employee pays 20 percent toward the changes for a service and the employer or insurance company pays 80 percent. This must be paid by the client. If you try to waive this fee and write the amount off as an expense it is considered insurance fraud. Many companies will have this contingency specified in their contracts.

Complementary and Alternative Medicine (CAM) – A term used to describe massage therapy, acupuncture and other non-traditional healing methods. http://nccam.nih.gov/health/whatiscam/

Concurrent care- If the client visits two health care providers that bill for the same service on any given day, the procedures are considered to be duplicate and will not be allowed (paid). For example: a client gets a massage and visits the physical therapist on the same day and they both bill 97140 – one of the providers will not get paid.

Conversion Factor – Conversion factors take into consideration geographical variations, inflation and variations in medical expenses. The conversion factors are then applied to the Relative Value Unit (RVU) to determine a price close to the usual, customary and reasonable charges. See also Relative Value Unit.

Co-Payment- Co-payment is a predetermined (flat) fee that an individual pays for health care services, in addition to what the insurance covers. For example, some HMOs require a $10 "co-payment" for each office visit, regardless of the type or level of services provided during the visit. Co-payments are not usually specified by percentages. When it is a percentage it is called a co-insurance payment

CPT code (Current Procedural Terminology) – 5 digit code indicating the procedure that you are performing on the client set up by the Physicians Current Procedural Terminology coding system and published by the American Medical Association.

Deductible -The amount an individual must pay for health care expenses before insurance (or a self-insured company) covers the costs. Often, insurance plans are based on yearly deductible amounts. The client will have to pay their medical expenses until that amount is met and then the insurance company will pay the benefits that are allowed in their policies.

Denial Of Claim- Refusal by an insurance company to honor a request by an individual (or his or her provider) to pay for health care services obtained from a health care professional.

Deposition –An out-of-court testimony made under oath and recorded by an authorized officer for later use in court or the meeting at which such testimony is taken. The attorneys will ask questions of the providers of health care in the case to obtain information necessary to settle the case. You may be asked to provide such information on any case you work on.

Diagnosis – The providing physician must provide a diagnosis and identify what disease, symptoms or illness a client has. Massage Therapists are not allowed to diagnose.

Diagnosis Code - A code determined by the World Health Organization for each specific diagnosis. Also known as an International classification of Diseases (ICD –9). The 9 refers to the 9th edition. Published annually by the Health Care Financing Administration (HCFA).

For a list of ICD-9 codes, see the appendix. ICD-9 codes should be supplied by the physician. I am only supplying the codes so that you can know what the diagnosis is when the physician supplies the code but not the written diagnosis. ICD-10 codes must be used on all HIPAA transactions, including outpatient claims with dates of service, and inpatient claims with dates of discharge on and after October 1, 2013. https://www.cms.gov/ICD10/

Disability – A person who is unable to work part or full time.

Disability Insurance – Private insurance that covers a person who is disabled until they are able to go back to work.

Documentation – The process of charting the progress or lack of progress of clients which will include SOAP chart notes.

Electronic Claim – Bills sent electronically through FAX or computer to the insurance company.

Employer self- insured plans – Insurance programs set up by companies for their employees by themselves rather than with a commercial insurance carrier. They often contract with a commercial insurance company to be the administrators. Companies who are self-insured usually do not have to abide by the same rules for coverage. Self insured companies here in WA State do not have to enforce the "Every Category Law" that allows massage therapists to become providers for HMO's and PPO's.

ERISA- Employee Retirement Insurance Security Act: Federal Act that regulates self-insured employers. They do not recognize massage therapists at this time.

Evaluation and Management Codes (E&M codes) – CPT codes that cover evaluating and managing a client's case. It is questionable as to whether or not massage therapists are allowed to use these codes. Ask the claims manager or adjuster if you are allowed to use this code. Some insurance companies in WA State allow therapists to bill these codes so make sure to ask.

Exclusions - Medical services that are not covered by an individual's insurance policy.

Explanation of Benefits (EOB) –An explanation of services issued to providers and patients telling them what has been paid, what is owing, how much the co-pay is, what has not and why not and for what dates of service.

Fee schedule – listing of established allowances set by the insurance companies; maximum allowable charge for specific medical services.

Also: the set fees or prices of the health care provider. It is important to have a fee schedule in written form.

Functional Goals/ Functional Outcomes, Functional Outcomes Reporting see: Hands Heal: Communication, Documentation, and Insurance Billing for Manual Therapists" by Diana L. Thompson for her interpretation of these terms.

Gatekeeper – The primary care physician (PCP)- Co-ordinates medical care in a managed care system.

Health Care Decision Counseling- Services, sometimes provided by insurance companies or employers that help individuals weigh the benefits, risks and costs of medical tests and treatments. Unlike case management, health care decision counseling is non-judgmental. The goal of health care decision counseling is to help individuals make more informed choices about their health and medical care needs, and to help them make decisions that are right for the individual's unique set of circumstances.

HCFA – Health Care Financing Administration – Department of Health and Human Services division that oversees federal health care regulations such as Medicare, Medicaid now known as the **Centers for Medicare & Medicaid Services** (**CMS**)

Health Maintenance Organizations (HMO's)- Health Maintenance Organizations represent "pre-paid" or "capitated" insurance plan in which individuals or their employers pay a fixed monthly fee for services, instead of a separate charge for each visit or service. The monthly fees remain the same, regardless of types or levels of services provided. Services are provided by physicians who are employed by, or under contract with, the HMO. HMOs vary in design. Depending on the type of the HMO, services may be provided in a central facility, or in a physician's own office.

ICD-code- International Classification of Disease code – A code that indicates what the diagnosis or condition is that the patient is being treated for. This is provided by the referring physician or health care provider. ICD-9 indicates the 9th edition. ICD –10 indicates the 10th edition. Codes are revised with each edition.

Independent Medical Exam (IME) –The examination of the client and their records by an independent party. In a personal injury case, the adjuster will usually call for an IME when they are determining if the service is reasonable and necessary. The insurance company pays for the exam. The doctor must be the same kind of provider as the PCP or doctor who referred the client for treatment. In general, when this exam is called for you can expect the benefits to be terminated. It is advisable that the client consult with the attorney before going to an IME and when the benefits are terminated.

Insured- The person who is the policyholder. This may not necessarily be the owner and it may not always be the injured party. The insured may be a spouse, dependent or a passenger.

Interim Report – A re-evaluation of the client's condition requested by the lawyer, insurance company or doctor.

Labor and Industry (L&I) or worker's compensation – Insurance Plan that covers workers on the job. Each state has different rules and regulations.

Lien – The process of filing a claim against the settlement to secure payment for your services. It may be a court document or a legal agreement between you and the client and their lawyer. Find out who you need to file this with by contacting the county court. You will have to remove the lien if filed with the courts as it will affect the client's credit report.

Medically necessity- Services such as massage therapy that may be need for treatment of the condition or illness. In order to bill insurance companies, the work you do must be medically necessary. The injury or illness must be diagnosed by a physician. Each company has their own definition of medically necessity.

Managed Care- A medical delivery system that attempts to manage the quality and cost of medical services that individuals receive. Most managed care systems offer HMOs and PPOs that individuals are encouraged to use for their health care services. Some managed care plans attempt to improve health quality, by emphasizing prevention of disease.

Maximum Dollar Limit- The maximum amount of money that an insurance company (or self-insured company) will pay for claims within a specific time period. Maximum dollar limits vary greatly. They may be based on or specified in terms of types of illnesses or types of services. Sometimes they are specified in terms of lifetime, sometimes for a year.

Mediation – Method of Alternate Dispute Resolution (ADR) in which the mediator acts as a liaison between the insurance company and the injured party to agree on a settlement. The mediator is paid by the parties requesting the mediation. You may be asked to appear at the mediation and report on your findings and treatments.

Modalities – For the purpose of insurance billing a modality uses mechanical devices or other methods to assist in the treatment; such as hot or cold packs, paraffin baths, infrared treatments.

Modalities are also a term used to describe the many different types of techniques of massage and bodywork. Different modalities are Reiki, Trigger point therapy, myofascial release, structural integration (there are literally hundreds).

Narrative Report – Summary of client's injuries, treatments given, and progress usually in a letter format. Often required for settlement.

Out-Of-Plan/out of network- This phrase usually refers to physicians, hospitals or other health care providers who are considered non-participants in an insurance plan (usually an HMO or PPO). Depending on an individual's health insurance plan, expenses incurred by services provided by out-of-plan health professionals may not be covered, or covered only in part by an individual's insurance company.

Palliative Care – Maintenance massage.

Pending Claim – Claim sent to insurance company that is being held for any number of reasons such as incorrect codes, or incomplete forms.

Personal Injury Protection (PIP) – A component of auto insurance that pays the medical bills directly before the case is settled. They will deal with getting the money from the responsible party later.

Pre-existing Conditions- A medical condition that is excluded from coverage by an insurance company, because the condition was believed to exist prior to the individual obtaining a policy from the particular insurance company.

Preferred Provider Organizations (PPO)- You or your employer receive discounted rates if you use doctors from a pre-selected group. If you use a physician outside the PPO plan, you must pay more for the medical care.

Prescriptions- Formal referrals from appropriate health care providers that include the diagnosis, the diagnosis code, the treatment plan. A prescription is necessary to prove medical necessity.

Primary Care Provider (PCP)- A health care professional (usually a physician) who is responsible for monitoring an individual's overall health care needs. Typically, a PCP serves as a "quarterback" for an individual's medical care, referring the individual to more specialized physicians for specialist care.

Progress Report /Progress Notes – System of charting a client's progress and condition. These are usually in the form of SOAP notes, but you can use whatever works for you. There are many methods of reporting: interim reports, narrative reports, etc.

Provider - Provider is a term used for health professionals who provide health care services. Sometimes, the term refers only to physicians. Often, however, the term also refers to other health care professionals such as hospitals, nurse practitioners, chiropractors, physical therapists, massage therapists and others offering specialized health care services.

Reasonable and Customary Fees- The average fee charged by a particular type of health care practitioner within a geographic area. The term is often referred to by insurance companies as the amount of money they will approve for a specific test or procedure. If the fees are higher than the approved amount, the individual receiving the service is responsible for paying the difference. Sometimes, however, if an individual questions his or her physician about the fee, the provider will reduce the charge to the amount that the insurance company has defined as reasonable and customary.

Relative Value Unit (RVU)- The assigned value of a CPT code that is relative to the actual costs of providing a procedure. Each insurance company takes each value and then multiplies it by the conversion factor for each specific region to determine an allowable fee or price for each code.

Resource Based Relative Value Scale (RBRVS) – system developed at Harvard University to assess health care providers work, overhead costs and malpractice risk for each CPT code.

Third Party Payment – Money paid by someone other than the person receiving the services or the primary provider, such as the insurance company of the person who is at fault for a motor vehicle accident.

Usual, Customary and Reasonable (UCR) or Covered Expenses-Set by the insurance companies to determine what to pay for each CPT code: An amount customarily charged for or covered for similar services and supplies which are medically necessary, recommended by a doctor, or required for treatment. The UCR is determined by services such as Medicode and published in the National Fee Analyzer.

Resources:

You can download the forms from my website at

http://thebodyworker.com/massage_insurance_billing_forms.htm

Cost per client formula

ICD-9 codes

Insurance Benefits verification form

Track insurance company communications

Intake forms

Physicians' referral/prescription

Insurance Billing and payment Tracking

Progress Report

Resources for billing

Cost per client formula:

Compute your office overhead for a month:

You can take the last 12 months and divide by 12. If you haven't been working for a year, you can estimate using numbers from the time you have worked.

	Sample	
Salary/needed income	$4000	
Rent	$600	
Other salaries		
Office expenses	$150	
Office Supplies	$50	
Marketing	$200	

Other expenses		
Total Expenses per month	$5000	

Compute the number of patients for the month. You can use last years patients divided by 12 or estimate the number for this year.

Sample: 15 clients per week x 4.2 weeks/mo = 63 clients per month

Cost per patient = Total monthly expenses____ divided by Total monthly patient visits

Sample: $5,000 ÷ 63 = $79.00

This is what your cost per patient is.

Evaluate

If you expect the number of clients to go up per month by 21 (5 per week) your cost per client will go down.

$5000 ÷ 84 = 59.52

$59.52 will be your new cost per client.

What is the amount that the insurance company will be paying you?

Less than that or more than that?

Will it be worth it to take on new clients at that expected rate?

Will you get too many clients that you will have to hire office support to do the extra work involved? Hiring someone will increase your expenses and increase the cost per client.

Insurance Benefits Verification Form

Patient Name _____

Address_____

Social Security #_____ date of birth_____

Work phone_____ home phone_____

Referring Physician_____

Insurance Information:

Insured's name:_____

Insured's Date of Birth:_____ Insured's SS#_____

Address:_____

Work phone: _____ home phone_____

Social security number_____

Claim number or ID number_____

Group number_____

Allowable benefits:_____

Yearly deductible :_____ Has it been met?_____

Co-pay_____

Name of person you talked to at your insurance company_____

Date and time of conversation:_____

Track communications with the insurance company

Patient : _____

Patient ID number/claim number _____

Issue _____
_____
_____

Resolution: _____
_____

What the insurance company will do:
_____
_____
_____

What you need to do:
_____
_____
_____

Follow up scheduled for:
_____

Person you spoke with: _____

Date and time you spoke with person: _____

Notes:

Confidential   Health   Intake   Form

Name _____ Date of Birth _____

Street Address _____

City_____ State_____ Zip_____

Wk. Phone _____ Hm.phone_____ CellPhone_____

Emergency Contact _____

Employer _____ Social Security Number _____

Occupation/employer _____

Referring Physician:_____ Primary Care Physician:_____

Was Injury a result of an accident?_____

If   yes: Job   related_____ Auto   _____

Other_____

Date of Injury or onset: _____

Insurance   Company

Name:_____

Billing Address:_____

Phone Number:_____

Contact person/ case manager _____

Name of Insured :_____ Insured's date of birth_____

Address:_____

Phone:_____

Group/Claim Number/Id number:_____

Insured'sss#_____

Attorney (if applicable) Name :_____

Address:_____ Phone number: _____

I hereby authorize the release of medical information necessary to process my insurance claim. This may include intake forms, chart notes, reports, correspondences, billing statements and any other information to my attorneys, health care providers and insurance case managers.

I am responsible for all charges for all services provided. In the event that the insurance company denies benefits or makes a partial payment, I am responsible for any balance due. This may not apply to insurance companies that I am under contract with. I understand the benefits and risks of massage and give my consent for massage. I will consult my practitioner with any questions or concerns immediately. I have stated all medical conditions that I am aware of and will keep my practitioner informed of any changes.

I agree to provide **24 hour** cancellation notice. If I fail to do so, I agree to pay the **full** appointment fee.
(Please note that insurance companies **do not** pay this, you do.)

Signature _____ Date _____

Medical History and Information

Check any or all that apply to your present health:

___ headaches ___chronic pain ___varicose veins

___ vision problems ___muscle or joint pain ___blood clots

___ sinus problems ___numbness/tingling ___high/low blood pressure

___ jaw pain/teeth grinding ___sprains/strains ___diabetes

___ fatigue ___scoliosis ___cancer/tumors

___ depression ___arthritis ___infectious disease

___ sleep difficulties ___tendonitis ___skin problems

Women only: ___Pregnant___ Painful menstruation___ endometriosis

Men only: ___Prostrate problems

List all medications/herbs/vitamins and dosage: _____
List physical activities you participate in regularly _____

What movements or activities are limited? _____

Describe the events of the injury or accident: _____

List previous major injuries/surgeries: _____
What other treatments are you receiving and by whom
(acupuncture, physical therapy, chiropractic, naturopathic): _____

What seems to help the most? _____

What seems to aggravate the condition the most? _____

What is your main activity at work?
On phone _____ Sitting _____ Computer work _____

Driving car _____ Walking _____ Other _____

What do you do to relieve stress? _____

What do you want to get out of you session (s) _____

Confidential Client Intake Form

Last Name(2) _____ First Name _____ MI ____

Address (5) _____

City _____ State _____ Zip _____

SS# ____ ____ _____ Birthday (3) ___/___/___ Circle: M F

Home Phone _____ Office Phone _____

Referred By (17) _____

Dr. Phone _____

Emergency Contact Name _____ Phone Number _____

Status (8) Single _____ Married _____ Other _____

Employed _____ Full-Time Student _____ Part-Time Student _____

Condition Related to (10)a. Employment (Y) (N)

b. Auto Accident (Y) (N) c. Other accident (Y) (N)

Insured's I.D. (if different from client) # (1a) _____ ____

Insured's Name (4) Last _____ First _____ M.I. ____

Address (7) _____

City _____ State _____ Zip _____

Insured's Policy or Group Number (11) _____

Insured's D.O.B. (a) ____/____/_____

Employer's Name (b) _____

Insurance Plan Name (c) _____

Is there another health benefit plan? (d) Y ____ N ____ (If yes, fill out below)

Other insured's name (9) Last _____ First _____ MI ____

Other Insured's policy or group # (a) _____ D.O.B. (b) ___/___/___

Sex: M ___ F ___

Employer's Name (c) _____ Insurance Plan Name (d) _____

The responsibility for the cost for each massage therapy session is the client's. Whatever portion of the session(s) not covered by a third party payer is the client's responsibility. Release (12) : Authorized signature: I authorize the release of any medical or other information necessary to the medical treatment of my condition and to process this claim. I also request payment of medical benefits either to myself or to this medical provider.

Signature_____Date_____

Physician Diagnosis(21)_____ ICD 9_____

Physicians Referral for Massage Therapy Services

From:_____	Condition is related to ___MVA___work injury
Patient Name:_____	___Other injury ___Stress ___other medical condition
Address:_____	Number of sessions to be done: (frequency and duration)_____
SS#_____	
Date of Birth:_____	Send progress report:
Insurance Company:_____	____ every week
Policy Number:_____	____every two weeks
Claim Number:_____	____at the completion of prescribed treatments
Billing Address:_____	____other_____
	Special directions/Comments:
Date of Injury:_____	_____
Diagnosis/ICD-9 code(s):_____	

reas to be worked on: (circle all that apply, add comments)

Cranial: Temporalis, Masseter, Frontalis_____

Cervical: E.S, Levator, Scalenes, SCM, Spenius Cervicus/Capitis, Trapezius, Sub-occipitals_____

Thoracic: E.S, Rhomboid, Serratus Anterior, Trapezius, Serratus posterior
superior_____

Shoulder: Infraspinatus, Supraspinatus, Subscapularis, Teres , Deltoid, PecMj,
PecMn_____

Lumbar: E.S, Quadratus, Iliacus,
Psoas_____

Sacral: Gluteus Max, Min, Med, Rotators, IT Band, Quads, Hamstrings,
TFL_____

Other:_____

Hydrotherapy: None, Heat, Cold
Location:_____

Physicians
Signature_____Date:_____

Physicians Name
printed:_____

Address_____

Phone_____

Insurance Billing and Payment Tracking

Billing Date	Ins. Co.	Dates of service	Co-pay	Amount billed	Amount paid	Payment date

Subjective and Objective Observations

	Left	Right	No Current Problem	Improving	Not Improving	↑Symptoms
Neck						
Shoulder						
Arm						
MidBack						
L.Back						
Pelvis						
Leg						

Patient rates their stress level as: ___Low___Moderate ___HighOther Concerns/Comments:_____
Thank You Very Much for your referral.

Online Resources:

www.sohnen-moe.com : Cherie Sohnen-Moe, author of "Business Mastery". Offers free forms on her website for all aspects of business building.

www.massageinsurancebilling.com – Vivian Madison- Mahoney: Comprehensive Guide to Insurance Billing; author of column on insurance billing in www.massagetoday.com

ICD 9 codes -http://thebodyworker.com/insbillcodes.html

National Association of Insurance Commissioners -www.**naic**.org/

Workers Compensation Departments
-http://www.dol.gov/owcp/dfec/regs/compliance/wc.htm

Books:

Hands Heal by Diana Thompson

Interviewing for solutions – Peter DeJong

Business Mastery- Cherie Sohnen-Moe

The Medical Massage Office Manual for Insurance Billing- David Luther, Margery Callahan

Comprehensive Guide to Insurance Billing – Vivian Madison Mahoney

Index

1099 form..............................76
97122 - Therapeutic procedure 53
97124 - Therapeutic procedure 53
97140 - Manual Therapy.......53
Affinity Plans.................40, 42
Affordable Healthcare Act.....5
Allowable Fee.......................91
Alternate Dispute Resolution 102
Arbitration............................92
Assessment...........................59
Centers for Medicare and Medicaid Services.............46
chain of trust........................20
CMS-1500......................46, 47
contracted provider..3, 4, 9, 34, 40, 42, 84
cost per client....10, 13, 15, 110
credentialing...............4, 40, 42
Current Procedural Terminology.......................................3
Dates of Service....................49
Deductible............................96
diagnosis 16, 35, 49, 54, 59, 60, 63, 65, 71, 75, 77, 97, 100, 104
Discount plans......................42
ERISA..................................98
Every Category Law..2, 40, 87, 98
Explanation of Benefits.........99
Fee schedule.........................99

functional outcomes 58, 59, 60, 92
Health Insurance Portability and Accountability Act....20, 94
HIPAA.................................20
ICD-10......................52, 55, 97
ICD-9.....10, 16, 49, 52, 54, 75, 97, 100, 107, 119
Indemnity plans....................33
Independent Medical exam (IME)................................38
informed consent form.........22
International Classification of Disease codes....................52
Issues in Coverage for Complementary and Alternative Medicine Services..............88
Labor & Industries................31
Labor and Industries 34, 44, 57, 73, 74, 93
Lien...............................78, 101
managed care....33, 40, 99, 102
Managed Care Plans.............33
massage research..................69
Med-Pay (MP)......................32
Medicaid.....33, 34, 46, 94, 100
medically necessary.......31, 56, 102, 106
Medicare......28, 33, 34, 46, 94, 100
Motor Vehicle accidents (MVA),..............................31
Narrative Report...................62

National Provider Identification Number (NPI)..................................23
Notification of Privacy Policies..............................21
Palliative Care....................103
Personal injury protection (PIP)..................................32
Place of Service....................49
Plan...60
Preferred Provider...31, 33, 84, 104
prescription..18, 35, 41, 42, 45, 54, 61, 63, 65, 71, 75, 77, 84, 104, 107
Primary Care Physician........84
referral network....................68
Relative Value Unit.............105
Self Insured Plans.................43
set your fees....................29, 30
Slip and Fall accidents..........39

SOAP charts.........................57
statement of privacy.............21
Subjective.............................57
Supervision...........................80
Third party coverage............32
Type of Service....................50
Uninsured motorists.............33
Uninsured Motorists Protection 39
Usual, Customary and Reasonable (UCR)................26, 106
Verify Benefits.....................74
W-2 form..............................76
website.2, 6, 21, 22, 23, 26, 67, 69, 71, 107, 123
Worker's compensation.31, 34, 44
Worker's compensation (WC) 31
'willingly' paying.................40

If you liked this book, please take a minute to review it on amazon.com. In return, I would be happy to send you a PDF Copy of this book that you can share with others and teach them how to bill or use for yourself to be able to access all of the links more easily from your computer. Please send me an email and tell me or show me your review. I appreciate it!

Please also join me at

www.facebook.com/MassagePracticeBuilder and ask any questions you have about billing or find information in the Forum

-www.massagepracticebuilder.com/forum

I also am looking for and appreciate any other feedback or comments. Please use the form below:

Feedback form

Please provide feedback about this Insurance Billing Manual

Copy and paste these questions into an email or send your own comments or feedback.

Send your response to julie@massagepracticebuilder.com

Did you find the information helpful? Accurate?
What other questions do you have regarding insurance billing procedures?
Have you found other questions that are necessary to ask insurance companies about their system?

Are you getting Paid ?

What issues have you been faced with?

Julie Onofrio, LMP

www.masagepracticebuilder.com

www.massagecareerguides.com

www.thebodyworker.com

©March, 2012

About the Author

Julie Onofrio, LMP is a massage therapist in Seattle WA and creator of many websites for the massage profession. You can connect with her at www.facebook.com/MassagePracticeBuilder or visit one of her many websites listed above.

Made in the USA
Lexington, KY
24 September 2012